# THE
# ANALYST
## AND THE
# RABBI

A Play by
## MURRAY STEIN
and
## HENRY ABRAMOVITCH

CHIRON PUBLICATIONS • ASHEVILLE, NORTH CAROLINA

www.ChironPublications.com

Interior and cover design by Danijela Mijailovic
Printed primarily in the United States of America.
We are grateful for permission to use this cover photo from the Eranos Archives.

ISBN 978-1-63051-732-8 paperback
ISBN 978-1-63051-733-5 hardcover
ISBN 978-1-63051-734-2 electronic
ISBN 978-1-63051-735-9 limited edition paperback

Library of Congress Cataloging-in-Publication Data

Names: Stein, Murray, 1943- author. | Abramovitch, Henry, 1950- author.
Title: The analyst and the Rabbi : a play / a play by Murray Stein and Henry Abramovitch.
Description: Asheville, North Carolina : Chiron Publications, 2020. | Includes bibliographical references. | Summary: "A meeting between C.G. Jung and Rabbi Leo Baeck took place in Zurich in October 1946 at the Savoy Hotel Baur en Ville. Very little is actually known about this meeting. There are no extant notes or reports from the principals indicating what was said or discussed. There was no secretary present taking down minutes of the conversation. What is known from the few documents attesting to this meeting is that it took place at Jung's request and that Baeck did not wish to meet with Jung. The play is an imaginative construction of what might have happened in this historic meeting of two great men"-- Provided by publisher.
Identifiers: LCCN 2020016281 (print) | LCCN 2020016282 (ebook) | ISBN 9781630517328 (paperback) | ISBN 9781630517335 (hardcover) | ISBN 9781630517342 (ebook).
Subjects: LCSH: Jung, C. G. (Carl Gustav), 1875-1961--Drama. | Baeck, Leo, 1873-1956--Drama.
Classification: LCC PS3613.U85 A53 2020 (print) | LCC PS3613.U85 (ebook) | DDC 812/.6--dc23
LC record available at https://lccn.loc.gov/2020016281
LC ebook record available at https://lccn.loc.gov/2020016282

# Table of Contents

# Introduction

"The Analyst and the Rabbi" is a work of imagination. However, it is based on a documented event—a meeting between C.G. Jung and Rabbi Leo Baeck that took place in Zurich in October 1946 at the Savoy Hotel Baur en Ville. Very little is actually known about this meeting. There are no extant notes or reports from the principals indicating what was said or discussed. There was no secretary present taking minutes of the conversation. What is known from the few documents attesting to this meeting is that it took place at Jung's request and that Baeck did not wish to meet with Jung.

Baeck did not want to meet with Jung for reasons that are stated in the play. Jung's reputation among Jews was deeply compromised because of statements he had made about "Jewish psychology" in an article titled "The State of Psychotherapy Today," published in 1934 in the *Zentralblatt für Psychotherapie und ihre Grenzgebiete* for which he was General Editor at the time. Sentences from this article are quoted in the play. The article itself is included in Volume 10 of *The Collected Works of C.G. Jung*. Further criticism arose because he had accepted the role of presidency of the International General Medical Society for Psychotherapy just at the time of Hitler's rise to power in 1933 and had continued to serve in that position through the 1930s. The organization was dominated in 1933 by the strong German branch of the Society, which was headed by the

Adlerian analyst Dr. Matthias Heinrich Göring, a cousin of the *Reichsmarschall*. Jung's reputation had been further tarnished by a public dispute in a Zurich newspaper between himself and Dr. Gustav Bally, who was actually a friend of Jung's, concerning his views of what was happening in Germany. Baeck had been a prominent rabbi in Germany at the time and during the war had spent several years in the concentration camp Theresienstadt. Recently freed from the camp, he was traveling in Europe to work on the restoration of the remaining Jewish communities. This brought him to Switzerland in 1946. Although he had known and admired Jung before the days of the Third Reich (see his letter to Jung in the Appendix), he was in no mood to meet a man who had since then become identified as a Nazi sympathizer.

Jung for his part at the time felt horribly misunderstood by those who identified him as an anti-Semite and a Hitler sympathizer. Serious accusations against him were circulating in America and elsewhere, and he was under pressure to explain his words and actions. When he heard that Rabbi Baeck was in Switzerland, he invited him to his home for a friendly meeting, possibly hoping to explain himself and perhaps to achieve reconciliation with his former admirer. When his invitations went unanswered, he took the initiative to go to the hotel in Zurich where Baeck was staying and ask to speak with him. What happened when they met at the Savoy Hotel is unknown. We only know that something took place that brought Rabbi Baeck to change his view of Prof. Jung.

The evidence for this change is contained in a letter written by the famous scholar of Jewish mysticism Gershom

Scholem to Aniela Jaffé, who was Jung's secretary at the time of his death and the collaborator in the authorship of Jung's autobiography, *Memories, Dreams, Reflections*. In his later years, Jung had become deeply interested in Kabbalah and had read Scholem's classic work, *Major Trends in Jewish Mysticism*. In response, he arranged to have Scholem invited to present a lecture at the annual gathering of eminent international scholars at the Eranos Conference Center in Ascona, Switzerland, but Scholem was uncertain whether to accept this invitation because of reports he had heard about Jung's purported anti-Semitic writings and attitudes. It was just at this point that Scholem met Rabbi Baeck, who had recently arrived in Palestine from Switzerland and from the meeting with Jung. In reply to a request from Aniela Jaffé asking about the meeting between Jung and Baeck, Scholem wrote::[1]

Jerusalem 7 May 1963

Dear Mrs. Jaffé:

> As you are so interested in the story of Baeck and Jung, I will write it down for your benefit and have no objection to being cited by you in this matter. In the summer of 1947 Leo Baeck was in Jerusalem. I had then just received for the first time an invitation to the Eranos meeting in Ascona, evidently at Jung's suggestion, and I

---

[1] Aniela Jaffé (1989) *From the Life and Work of C.G. Jung*, Einsiedeln: Daimon Verlag, p. 100.

asked Baeck whether I should accept it, as I had heard and read many protests about Jung's behavior in the Nazi period. Baeck said: "You must go, absolutely!" and in the course of our conversation told me the following story. He too had been put off by Jung's reputation resulting from those well-known articles in the years 1933-34, precisely because he knew Jung very well from the Darmstadt meetings of the School of Wisdom and would never have credited him with any Nazi and anti-Semitic sentiments. When, after his release from Theresienstadt, he returned to Switzerland for the first time (I think it was 1946), he therefore did not call on Jung in Zurich. But it came to Jung's ears that he was in the city and Jung sent a message begging him to visit him, which he, Baeck, declined because of those happenings. Whereupon Jung came to his hotel and they had an extremely lively talk lasting two hours, during which Baeck reproached him with all the things he had heard. Jung defended himself by an appeal to the special conditions in Germany but at the same time confessed to him: "Well, I slipped up"- probably referring to the Nazis and his expectation that something great might after all emerge. This remark, "I slipped up," which Baeck repeated to me several times, remains vividly in my memory. Baeck said that in this talk they cleared up everything that had come between them and that they parted from one another reconciled again. Because of this explanation of Baeck's I accepted the invitation to Eranos when it came a second time.

Yours sincerely,

G. Scholem

This is the only document in existence about Jung's meeting with Baeck in Zurich. The date of the meeting can be inferred from the two brief invitations sent to Baeck by Jung's secretary at the time (see Appendix).

"The Analyst and the Rabbi" is an attempt to imagine what might have happened there, what was said, and how the dialogue evolved from suspicion and mistrust to reconciliation. One key point rests upon the English translation of the German expression, "*Ich bin ausgerutscht,*" which is how Jung is quoted in Scholem's German language letter to Jaffé. The English translation has Jung saying, "I slipped up," which makes his apology sound rather flippant and unconvincing. In German, it sounds more serious and could be translated instead as "I slipped off the path," which in the Swiss Alps is significant indeed. It is this translation that we use in the play. Otherwise, it would not be credible that Baeck would have taken Jung's apology seriously.

The backstory of how this play came into being might be of interest.

I (Murray) came to Israel in 2015 at the invitation of the Israel Institute of Jungian Psychology. I preferred not to give a formal lecture but asked rather that my colleague, Henry Abramovitch, dialogue with me in front of a public audience. This was well received, and the next day Henry took me and my wife, Jan, to Masada to see the sights of the famous citadel where the Jews held out heroically against the Romans some 2,000 years before. Strolling across the grounds of this magnificent old palace of Herod the Great, we discovered that we had both studied at Yale University around the same time. Henry reminisced to me about how much he had been involved in drama during his undergraduate days as actor, director, and playwright, and at that point I turned to him and announced with some considerable excitement, "You are the man!" I told him that I had been thinking about writing a play about the encounter between Jung and Baeck and was looking for a collaborator who knew more than I did about Baeck and his Jewish background. I wasn't sure how a man like Baeck would conduct himself and speak in such a tense situation. Henry accepted enthusiastically. It was a partnership confirmed with a handshake and made, so to say, in a heavenly realm high up and above the Dead Sea.

The collaboration was not without its challenges, however. Although we are good colleagues and both trained Jungian analysts, we live in different countries (Israel and Switzerland), and neither of us had ever written a play before. Over a period of three years, we communicated via email and Skype, and Henry once visited me for an intensive weekend of plotting and imagining. By the time we were satisfied with a draft ready to be rehearsed, we had gone through perhaps 100 revisions. Some of the texts we consulted and used in our research are listed in the bibliography.

In the "Dialogue Between the Authors" (see below), we reflect on our collaboration and its meaning. It has been an adventure in thinking with imagination and a creative experience for both of us.

We must acknowledge, too, that the ensemble of actors from the International School of Analytical Psychology in Zurich and Barbara Miller, a Jungian psychoanalyst from Holland as the musician in the production, have played an important role in shaping the play. With Paul Brutsche in the role of Prof. Jung, John Hill as Rabbi Leo Baeck, and Dariane Pictet as Woman, the spoken lines of the play were massaged gently into their present form. Barbara Miller contributed her professional musical knowledge by making the selection of musical pieces that are inserted at various points in the play, and her performance of these pieces was brilliant. The performance of the play that took place at the Foyer St. Anton in Zurich on October 29, 2018, was filmed by Luis Moris and his crew and is available on DVD from Chiron Publications.

Murray Stein and Henry Abramovitch

# The Analyst and the Rabbi – a Play

Characters in the Play

Prof. C.G. Jung ---- World famous Swiss psychiatrist and founder of Analytical Psychology

Rabbi Leo Baeck ---- A Leading Figure in the German Jewish Community before WWII, Author, Holocaust Survivor

Woman ---- A Mysterious Hovering Presence with Multiple Functions

All music in the play is played on the cello.

## *Scene 1*


Music: Vivaldi Cello Sonata #VI 46: 2 Largo
Curtain opens on a dimly lit stage. Woman stands
    alone toward back of stage. As music stops,
    Jung enters from stage left and light comes up
    on him. Woman moves to his side.

**Jung**: (Speaking defiantly, as if defending himself) But I am *not* guilty as charged!

**Woman**: You're still dwelling on that! Then maybe you *are*!

**Jung**: They're spreading such lies about me, that I was an agent of Hitler's! There is even a rumor that I'm hiding out somewhere in America and the FBI is investigating.

**Woman**: You *have* to speak with him. He's in town, staying at the Savoy Hotel. Maybe he can help. He is a rabbi. Maybe even a *tzaddik*, a righteous man.

**Jung**: Yes. I remember him well. I do wish he had accepted our invitation to have dinner at my place. It would have been so much easier.


Light off Jung and onto Baeck as he enters from
    stage right. Woman glides over to his side.


**Baeck**: (Speaks as though to himself) That Professor Jung! What chutzpah. Wanting to see me like we are old friends … and after what he wrote in the times of persecution.

**Woman:** But you know he was not a Nazi. Besides, he has so many Jewish friends and Jewish students.

**Baeck:** It doesn't matter. What he said was used savagely against us and was extremely damaging. How can I sit down with such a man?

**Woman:** You could meet him here at the hotel. You refused his invitations to Küsnacht, but this is a neutral place. Just to see what he wants. Could it hurt? Now, in 1946?

**Baeck:** This will not help my mission to restore the Jewish communities in Europe.

**Woman:** I don't think you have to worry about that.

Light off Baeck, back on Jung as Woman moves
over to Jung's side.

**Jung:** Dreams! Sometimes, I have to say, I hate them. They don't leave me in peace.

**Woman:** It's about her again, isn't it?

**Jung:** Yes … I dreamed about Sabina again. She was running frantically, naked, being chased by Gestapo troops dressed in black. Her daughters, too. They were running for their lives. The soldiers took aim and killed all three in cold blood. I was overwhelmed with anguish. Then that voice! It won't leave me alone.

**Woman:** What did the voice say?

**Jung:** Baeck. Go to Baeck. Visit Baeck. Like a broken record, repeating over and over again. Baeck. Baeck.

**Woman:** Well?

**Jung**: I wanted to argue, to ask some questions. No chance. You can't talk back to a disembodied voice. I have to answer to it.

**Woman**: Well?

**Jung**: Where is my coat? I've got to go and see him.

Music: Beethoven's String Quartet op. 18, #6,
"La Malinconia," Adagio. Woman moves
to Baeck. Light moves with her.

**Baeck**: I have a sense he is coming here. What will he say? What can I say? I don't want to lose my temper.

**Woman**: Why don't you….

**Baeck**: (Interrupting) Leave me alone!

**Woman**: You're still recovering. You need strength for this.

**Baeck**: But the nightmares! They keep coming back.

**Woman**: But there have been some changes, haven't there?

**Baeck**: There was one change. Last night, instead of the Nazi guard shooting my friend, David, a Russian soldier shot the guard. I couldn't help feeling glad. Maybe I should feel guilty…. But I just don't want to see him!

Music: Beethoven's String Quartet op. 18, #6,
"La Malinconia," Adagio

## Scene 2

Whole stage lit. Jung steps to center stage accompanied by Woman. Baeck stands at stage right. There is a wall (imaginary) between them, with a door.

**Jung**: (Knocks quietly on the door) Rabbi Baeck! It's Professor Jung. I would like to speak with you.

**Woman**: (After a pause) They told us at the desk downstairs that he's in. Knock again.

**Jung**: (Knocks louder) Hello! Rabbi Baeck! Please open the door. I want to speak with you.

**Woman**: OK, try one more time. If he doesn't answer after three knocks, he never will.

**Jung**: (Knocking louder) Rabbi Baeck, I beg you, please open the door.

**Baeck**: (From behind the door) What do you want?

**Jung**: I need to speak with you.

**Baeck**: (To himself) I do not want to speak with him, but he is outside my door. (Long pause … then he opens the door) Please enter.

**Woman**: (Moving forward) Finally they have come face to face, two tall men, both famous, both in their 70s, one a Gentile and one a Jew. They stand there stiff as boards. There is so much tension between them. They would like to leave, but they can't.

**Baeck**: (Reluctantly) Please take off your coat. We can sit here. (They remain standing.)

**Jung**: Thank you for allowing me in. It's been some time since we last met. I heard you were coming to Zurich. How are you?

**Baeck**: Let's not waste our time with niceties, Professor. What do you want? Why have you come here?

**Jung**: I want to explain. I want you to know that I'm not guilty as charged.

**Baeck**: (Surprised) Who charged you? What is the charge?

**Jung**: There are many vicious rumors floating around about me, spread by my enemies, that I was a Nazi and that I am anti-Semitic, even that I worked for Hitler. This is not true! I have done nothing to deserve this.

**Baeck**: (Firm and direct) I have *one* question for you, Professor Jung: Did you stand up to the great evil in that time, that everyone could see?

**Jung**: (Taken aback. A long, awkward pause) I have heard that you were in the camps. I would like to hear about your ordeal and how you survived.

**Baeck**: What you are asking of me is not easy to give, but I can tell you a few things and am prepared to listen to you. Do you remember my question?

**Woman**: (Aside to Jung) You are relaxing a little. That is good. (Aside to Baeck) You seem to be eying each other with less suspicion, but you have not yet let down your guards. Maybe a conversation will become more possible as you sit together. It would be so good if you could talk more freely with each other. (They pull two chairs to center stage and sit down.)

**Jung**: (As he sits down) May I respectfully ask you a question?

**Baeck**: (Silently nods)

**Jung**: Please tell me, Rabbi Baeck, which of my writings have you read, and what have you heard about me?

**Baeck**: I see no need for a lengthy recitation, Professor. My basic question is this: Why didn't you stand up and denounce Hitler when you knew so well, as the great psychologist you undoubtedly are, what a pathological and dangerous character he was and what a threat to humanity and civilization? Why didn't you speak up?

**Jung**: You are asking: Was I a coward? I have been accused of that, even by some of my best students like Erich Neumann. I have asked myself this question many times since being confronted in the Zurich newspaper by my friend Gustav Bally.

**Baeck**: A man of your stature should have spoken out publicly, and strongly, against what was happening in Germany, not only for Jews but also for psychiatric patients. Didn't you realize they were also being exterminated? How can you explain your silence?

**Jung**: (With some anger) I do find your tone quite harsh, Rabbi Baeck. I am human; I, too, have anxieties about my life and well-being. I also have other, you might call it, distracting interests. In those early years of Hitler's rule, I had some hopes that Germany would recover its place in the world after the devastation of the Great War. And I was not alone in this prospect.

**Baeck**: Many people chose to be naïve about Hitler and the Nazis. We, too, hoped they would soon disappear and life could get back to normal. You must know that many of us Jews were ardent German citizens and patriots. To Hitler, this, of course, was meaningless. Racism replaced patriotism. Suddenly we became outsiders, aliens. It was a shock, let me tell you, and it took us years to absorb and to believe it.

**Jung**: Why didn't you leave? Surely, there were many opportunities.

**Baeck**: (Stands up) I had no choice. I am a rabbi; I would never abandon my people, nor betray my vocation. It was my duty to stay.

Music: Vivaldi, "Cello Sonata #6," 2nd Largo

*As before, the two men sit facing one another.*
*Woman stands apart.*

**Woman:** (To Baeck, then to Jung) You are both remarkable men, exceptional in your achievements but separated by a deep rift, mistrustful of one another. Can you find a way to share your thoughts after these terrible years of suffering, betrayal, and trauma? What can become of this conversation?

**Baeck:** What *do* you want from me, Professor Jung?

**Jung:** I had to make contact with you. I'm not sure why. I had some dreams that directed me to see you. I had to come here. I had no choice. I came to explain, or so I thought, but now I'm not sure if that is the reason I'm here. Can we just talk for a bit? (Pulls chair closer)

**Baeck:** I wrote you a brief note after a lecture you gave in Darmstadt back in 1930. You had to rush away at the time. I remember that I said I appreciated what you had said and found it useful in my work.

**Jung:** And I never replied, but I always remembered it. Those were very busy days for me, Rabbi Baeck. I'm sorry I didn't write back to you.

**Baeck:** They were busy days for me, too, as you can imagine. I was president at the time of the German Rabbinical Association and had many duties to fulfill. Your name was well-known in Berlin, and some of your students were in my congregation. We looked to you in those days for psychological insight and guidance. So you can appreciate our deep shock and betrayal when you wrote so insensitively about "Jewish psychology" in 1934.

**Jung:** And I was president of an International Medical Psychotherapy Association at that time. I was asked to take that office, and against my better judgment, I accepted it out of a sense of responsibility. I was trying to help preserve psychotherapy in an increasingly hostile German nation. My German friends and colleagues begged me to take the post. I'm sure you can understand my dilemma. I would have greatly preferred to stay out of politics in neutral Switzerland.

**Baeck:** And might there be a different motive, as well?

**Jung:** What do you mean?

**Baeck:** I mean, Professor Jung, a motive that is a little less noble? Germany was a big prize, professionally speaking. Freud was now out, and you could step in.

**Jung:** (Stands up) Please hear me out, Rabbi Baeck. I was trying to make the case that there is more to psychology and psychotherapy than Freud and Adler. This was to protect the profession of psychotherapy, not to advance myself. Of course, this landed me in all kinds of hot water. As you say, I have been accused of trying to use this as an opportunity to put my psychology forward and gain an advantage over the Freudians. (A pause) Of course, I considered this, too, but it was never uppermost in my mind.

**Baeck:** Well?

**Jung**: Excuse me?

**Baeck**: Isn't it true that you used this opportunity to increase your presence in the professional world of Germany? This fell into your lap, and you used it.

**Jung**: Yes, that was the general view concerning Germany in the profession, but this was not my conscious and foremost intention. Of course, it did occur to me, in the back of my mind, that this put my psychological theory in a privileged position in Germany.

**Baeck**: As you might say, at the back of your mind in the shadow.

**Jung**: (Shifting uncomfortably in his chair) Yes, if you must press the matter so, I have to admit it.

**Woman**: (To herself) Things are moving forward now. Jung is beginning to sweat. This must be starting to feel like analysis. The rabbi is laying bare some hidden motivations. The conversation is becoming more real, less defensive. Jung is a proud man. This is very uncomfortable for him.

**Baeck**: I was in Berlin, Professor Jung, and I can tell you that the Nazis were thrilled to have you in the association. It gave them a big international name around the world and made them look legitimate. I found it more than difficult to explain your words to members of my congregation. Especially since I had been promoting your ideas. What could I say now? You wrote and I quote:

**Woman**: (Reading from the text "The State of Psychotherapy Today")

"The Jew who is something of a nomad has never yet created a cultural form of his own and as far as we can see never will, since all his instincts and talents require a more or less civilized nation to act as host for their development."

**Baeck:** (Stands up and paces as he speaks) How could you write that we Jews were parasites, unable to create our own culture but only living off the cultures of others? This was like something straight out of *Mein Kampf.* Didn't you understand how the Nazis would use your words about "Jewish psychology"?

**Jung:** In that article, I thought that by somehow partially allying myself with the German collective at that time, I could find a space to say some other things, to introduce some psychological reflections, to bring a little more consciousness to this nation possessed by rage and resentment.

**Baeck:** (With raised voice, emotional) Let me tell you something about "Jewish psychology," Professor Jung. We German Jews were unprepared for the rise of Nazis because we felt more German than the Germans, like two souls in one body. German and Jewish. Other nations feared the Germans, but as German Jews we loved *deutsche Kultur*, its *Dichter und Denker*. Every Jewish schoolboy knew his Goethe off by heart.

**Jung:** I must confess we were afraid of the Jews' success. To us, the Jews were a threat.

**Baeck:** So the Nazis made up a deceitful story to cover their resentment at our success. They screamed: "The Jews stabbed Germany in the back." Did you know the youngest volunteer in the German Army was Jewish, only 13 years old? And the first member of the German Parliament who volunteered for the front and died for the *Vaterland* was a Jew. 35,000 Jews were decorated for bravery. 12,000 died. May their memory be a blessing. I myself served as an army rabbi for all four years of the Great War. Then suddenly, in 1933, we were told we were aliens—vermin, a cancer in the body politic. Our rights were stripped from us. We were hunted down, robbed, terrorized, murdered.

**Woman**: (To herself) Jung looks like he has seen a ghost floating in the air between them.

**Jung**: Obviously, looking back, it was a mistake. I did not register the terror that you speak of. I was deafened by so many other voices.

**Baeck**: You're letting yourself off lightly, Professor Jung. That's a poor excuse. These statements you made will never be forgotten or forgiven.

**Woman**: (Reflectively) It's beginning to dawn on Jung how far he underestimated the seriousness of what he has done. He is finding it difficult to look the rabbi in the eye. He has nowhere to hide.

Music: Viktor Ullmann's opera, "Der Kaiser von Atlantis"

# Scene 4

The two men are seated; Woman in background.

**Baeck:** You know, Professor Jung, as I sit here at the Savoy in the comfort of this fine Swiss hotel in Zurich, I think of the contrast with the camp I lived in for three years, Theresienstadt. Do you know about it?

**Jung:** Yes, of course. It's north of Prague. I believe it was the site of the Nazi propaganda film we heard about during the war. There were some pictures in the newspapers.

**Baeck:** Then maybe you saw me there, listening to a lecture as if I was at Heidelberg. The truth was very different. At Theresienstadt, I was a horse. Every morning, while harnessed to a wagon with a fellow Jew, I dragged garbage and dead bodies through the streets. Not until I experienced it myself, with my own eyes, did I fully understand what it meant to live in one of these camps. Bunks were constructed in four or five decks, with so little space between them that you had to lean far forward when sitting upright so your head would be in the clear. The worst was the dirt, the teeming myriad of insects … and the gnawing hunger that never seemed to end. … The separation from loved ones was excruciating. Sometimes being together was even worse. Four of my sisters died at Theresienstadt: Frieda, Lisa, Anna and Rose. Kafka's sister; Freud's sisters. … Once when I had dysentery, I soiled myself waiting in line. … I lost 25 kilos.

**Jung**: How did you survive the humiliation, the suffering?

**Baeck**: Do you know the meaning of my family name—Baeck? It is an acronym of two Hebrew letters, *Beth* and *Kuf*. When spoken together it becomes "Baeck," a short form for "*ben kadosh*," meaning "son of holy ones, of the martyrs who died sanctifying the Holy Name." Only after I was arrested did I understand the meaning of my name, "Baeck," as my fate, my destiny. My name gives me strength.

**Jung**: *Ben Kadosh*. Baeck. Your name touches on ancient layers of the psyche. My name is rather new. Jung means "young." Maybe this explains how I got caught up in the excitement of a new wave of energy in Germany, a renewal of the collective spirit. A new leader had appeared, a figure of strength and determination. I was fascinated at first. We are now looking back in retrospect after the catastrophe. Our judgments were very different in 1933.

**Baeck**: (Sharply) I disagree. True, in 1933 no one knew the depth of the evil that lay ahead. We had no idea, no precedent. But we Jews certainly felt the deadly threat right from the beginning. There was a knife at our throats from the moment the Nazis came to power. This is where you lost your way, Professor Jung. You were blind and deaf to this threat to so many people in your neighboring country, Deutschland. You looked the other way.

**Jung**: (Silent, listening)

**Baeck:** You know, Professor, certain memories haunt me. November 9, 1938. Do you remember it?

**Jung:** Yes. The infamous *Kristallnacht.*

**Baeck:** I can see it clearly, as if illuminated by a flash bulb. I remember exactly where I stood. What I saw. What I smelled. After the shattering of the glass, a fearful silence lay over Berlin. *Kristallnacht.* But the silence began to speak. It carried a message.

**Jung:** (Listening in silence)

**Baeck:** It was difficult to know the right way to act. I made it a principle to accept no appointment from the Nazis, to do nothing to help them. But later when the question arose whether to allow Jewish orderlies to help pick up Jews for the transports, I took the position that it would be better for them to do it because they would at least be more gentle and careful than the Nazi police. When the Germans finally dissolved the Jewish fraternal organization, B'nai B'rith, they arrested me since I was the grandmaster. In prison, they demanded I sign over all B'nai B'rith property. I refused.

**Jung:** (Reflectively, in a whisper) In retrospect, I, too, should have refused. But I was confronted with terrible choices.

**Woman:** (To Jung) You seem to be peering into the abyss, Professor Jung.

**Baeck:** Let me remind you that your life did not depend on what you did or didn't do. My people's and mine did. I had no choice but to do my duty as best I could. I am a rabbi. (Stands) Each day I recited Psalm 56:

> Be merciful to me, my God,
>> for my enemies are in hot pursuit;
>> all day long they press their attack.
> My adversaries pursue me all day long;
>> in their pride many are attacking me.
> When I am afraid, I put my trust in you.

**Woman:** (Joining Baeck in remembering) We entered the camp …

**Baeck:** At Theresienstadt each of us received a transport number. This was the only sign of our existence. My number was 187984. This numbering system had the effect of officially deleting our personal identities, our names and histories, and threatened inwardly to cancel a feeling of self. We were as the dead. That was the mental battle we had to keep up, to see our fellow prisoners and ourselves not as transport numbers, but as persons.

**Jung:** How ever did you manage to maintain your sense of worth as human beings under those conditions?

**Baeck:** For one thing, I had a sense of the spiritual and intellectual hunger in the people around me. When Dutch Jews started arriving, I heard the Gestapo agent reading off their names.

**Woman:** (Remembering and calling the names of the new arrivals in a Gestapo-like voice): Asher, Meijers, de Levie, Frank, Benninga, Mesquita, Israel, Cohen, Gans, Tuscinski, da Costa…

**Baeck:** As I heard their names, I saw with my mind's eye the history of the whole Jewish Netherlands dating back to the 17th century. These people were intellectuals and scholars, artists and musicians.

**Jung**: (Listening intently)

**Baeck**: So then and there I decided to start a lecture series. We met at night in one of the barracks, in the heat of summer and the cold of winter, in the dark. With a little candlelight, I could make out some of their faces. In the freezing darkness sometimes hundreds of people jammed into the cold and gloomy attic, pressed close together for warmth, to hear a talk about Spinoza or the Talmud, Plato or the Bible, Aristotle or Isaiah. A sense of kinship arose up out of this mass of suffering. These were hours of freedom, which transformed us back into human beings. We also had choirs, opera, children's opera, original chamber music and even cabaret with its defiant jokes. My favorite joke was this one.

A Jewish father is teaching his son to say the blessing before meals: "Today in Germany the proper form of grace before our meals is: 'Thank you God and Hitler.'" "But suppose the Führer dies," the young boy asks his father.

"Then," his good father replies, "you just say, 'Thank you, God!'"

(Both laugh freely)

**Jung**: Even in the darkest hour ... laughter ...

**Woman**: (Reflectively) When the two men laugh together, their faces brighten. They begin to enjoy the company of one another. Still, the darkness prevails.

**Music:** Ullmann, from Theresienstadt

## Scene 5

Both men seated facing one another. Woman
behind. Lights up brightly.

**Jung**: Rabbi Baeck, you have gazed into the face of absolute evil.
Were you ever tempted to curse God and die?
**Baeck**: (Stands up) No, I was not. Every day, I said Kaddish over
bodies of people who had died.
(Chanted by Baeck and Woman as though over a gravesite)
*Glorified and sanctified be God's great name throughout
the world which He has created according to His will.*
*May He establish His kingdom in your lifetime and
during your days, and within the life of the entire House
of Israel, speedily and soon; and say, Amen.*
*May His great name be blessed forever and to all eternity.
Blessed and praised, glorified and exalted, extolled and
honored, adored and lauded be the name of the Holy One,*
**Woman and Baeck**: *Blessed be He,*
**Baeck**: *beyond all the blessings and hymns, praises and
consolations that are ever spoken in the world; and say,*
**Woman and Baeck**: *Amen.*
**Baeck**: *May there be abundant peace from heaven, and
life, for us and for all Israel; and say,*
**Woman and Baeck**: *Amen.*
**Baeck**: *He who creates peace in His celestial heights, may
He create peace for us and for all Israel; and say,*
**Woman and Baeck**: *Amen.*

**Jung:** *Amen!* When I hear this prayer for the dead, a shiver runs across my back and down my spine. I can see a light shining from your face as you speak the ancient words of the Kaddish prayer.

**Baeck:** To give people hope in those dark times, I would recite a passage from Ezekiel. (The three join in to speak these words of Ezekiel)

> **Woman:** *"Son of man, can these bones live?"*
>
> **Baeck:** *I said,*
>
> **Jung:** *"You know, oh Lord."*
>
> **Baeck:** *Then He said to me,*
>
> **Woman:** *"Prophesy to these bones and say to them,*
>
> **Jung:** *'Dry bones, hear the word of the Lord!*
>
> **Woman:** *This is what the Lord says to these bones:*
>
> **Baeck:** (his voice rising) *I will make breath enter you, and you will live.*
>
> **Woman:** (in a strong and determined voice) *I shall put sinews on you, I shall make flesh grow on you, I shall cover you with skin and I will put breath in you,*
>
> **Baeck:** *and you shall live ..."'*

**Jung:** I heard my grandfather speak this passage from Ezekiel in Hebrew. He was fluent in the ancient tongue and believed in the return of the Jews to the Holy Land.

**Baeck:** (After a pause, becoming agitated as he remembers) Do you know who was the camp commander of Theresienstadt, Professor Jung? His name was Sturmbannführer Rahm. His name, ironically, means "cream." Imagine. He was responsible for that infamous propaganda film showing Theresienstadt as a beautiful summer camp! After the film was made, he personally escorted one of the housemothers—who was in the film!—to the transport going directly to the Auschwitz gas chambers. He told the SS officer:

**Woman:** (Speaking for Rahm) "This is Mrs. Zucker. You are responsible for seeing that tonight she will be in her husband's arms."

**Baeck**: That was Rahm.

**Pause** (Both men look anxious, thinking back.)

Music: From Theresienstadt music by Ullmann

## Scene 6

Jung and Baeck are sitting. Woman stands next to Jung.

**Woman:** (To Jung) Perhaps it is the moment to tell Rabbi Baeck about your experience. He seems open to you.

**Jung:** Rabbi Baeck, your words have touched me in a profound way. I came to you, and you told me your story. Now there is something I must tell you. It's about an experience I had a couple of years ago. It occurred while you were in that hellish world of the camp and I was removed from daily life among family and with patients. It took place in a Zurich hospital. In this period, I believe I was brought close to you in some uncanny way. I will never forget it.

**Baeck:** (Silent, then with a nod of permission)

**Jung:** It was early 1944 and a very cold winter that year. The war was raging on, and the outcome was still in doubt. I slipped on the ice in the street and broke my leg. For some days I lay in the hospital. Then suddenly an embolism developed and made its way to my heart. For a time, I was at death's door. During the day I lay in a sort of half coma. I could not eat. I did not want to live. But at night I would revive a bit. Of course there were drugs involved to relieve the pain and to induce sleep. But instead of sleeping, I would become hungry and ask for food. And then things became very surreal. (Woman approaches Jung quietly.) The young nurse now took the form of a kind old Jewish woman. She brought me ritual kosher dishes. I was so grateful for her kindness and her loving presence. When I looked at her closely, and this is most strange, she had a blue halo around her head. (Stands up as though in a state of reverie)

**Woman**: (To Jung) Tell him your vision, what you see.

**Jung**: In this state, I myself was, so it seemed, in the Pardes Rimmonim, the garden of pomegranates, and the wedding of Tifereth with Malchuth was taking place. Or else I was Rabbi Simon ben Jochai, celebrating his wedding in the afterlife. It was the mystic marriage according to the Cabbalistic tradition. I cannot tell you how wonderful it was. I only kept thinking continually, "Now this is the garden of pomegranates! Now this is the marriage of Malchuth with Tifereth!" I do not know exactly what part I played in it. At bottom: I was the marriage. And my beatitude was that of a blissful wedding. (Comes out of his reverie and becomes alert again, looking at Baeck intently) Dear Rabbi, this experience changed me profoundly. And I think now that is why I came here today—to tell you this.

**Baeck**: Do you understand why you had these visions?

**Woman**: (To Jung) You are silent. Perhaps you understand and do not understand.

**Baeck**: (With urgency) Do you understand?

**Jung**: (Shakes his head) It is still somewhat dark to me, but I feel it so deeply. The mystic marriage touched me profoundly.

**Baeck**: Do you think this vision came to awaken your inner connection to the Jewish soul?

**Jung**: This must be true. Jewish features of my anima image have long fascinated me. My father knew Hebrew, and my grandfather spoke it. This Jewish part surprised me when I first discovered it in a relationship to a patient many years ago. And when I began to study the Kabbalah a few years ago, I could feel it. The vision must speak of my relationship to the Jewish soul.

**Baeck**: (After a pause) Listen, Professor Jung. There is something I need to tell.

**Jung:** Yes?

**Baeck:** And I am choosing to tell it to you.

**Jung**: I will listen as an analyst. It is in confidence.

**Baeck**: (Silent for a time.)

**Jung**: I am listening. Go ahead. (Leans forward to listen.)

**Baeck**: I need to speak about a decision I made… (Looks troubled, on the verge of tears)

**Jung**: Yes, go on …

**Baeck**: It's about a decision I made … in the gray zone.

**Jung**: In the gray zone?

**Baeck**: Where bad and good blend into each other and you can't tell them apart.

**Jung:** (Nods) Yes …

**Baeck**: In August of 1943, a year before the Red Cross visit and the filmmaking, a Czech engineer named Grünberg asked to speak with me … alone. He swore me to silence.

**Woman** (Speaks for Grünberg as the lights dim): Promise me you won't tell anyone. I have to tell this to someone. My best friend, who is half-Jewish, had been sent to the East, and he ended up in Auschwitz. He knows what goes on there. He knows what everyone at Auschwitz knows. He bribed a guard to get into Theresienstadt. He wanted to warn me and to save me.

**Baeck:** From that moment, I knew that Auschwitz was not just a rumor about being a death camp. I debated with myself: Was it was my duty to convince Grünberg to appear before the Jewish Council of Elders in Theresienstadt and tell them the truth?

**Jung:** To speak, or not to speak?

**Baeck:** Exactly. I realized that if the council were informed, the whole camp would know in a few hours. ... Living in expectation of death by gassing would be unbearable for the people.

**Jung:** But you also ...

**Baeck:** (Interrupting) I know what you will say, but please listen. I have been criticized for keeping silence. I had this horrible knowledge, but no arms, no underground organization, no weapons, no chance to put up a real fight in the camp. I had seen reprisals in Berlin. ... On our transports, if someone escaped, someone else was put in their place. ... Destroying hope is like murder, even more brutal than death in the gas chambers. If these people knew what the transports to the East really meant, would they have been able to hold out?

**Jung:** So you had to keep this terrible secret to yourself.

**Baeck:** (Pleading for understanding) You see, death was not absolutely certain for everyone. There was selection for slave labor; perhaps not all transports went to Auschwitz. Only ...

**Jung**: Only ...?

**Baeck**: I felt it was my duty, as a rabbi, to give my people hope. So I came to the grave decision...

**Jung**: To tell no one...

**Baeck**: To tell no one. The worst was that some people did come to me to ask whether they should go on the transports to the East.

**Woman**: (Stands before Baeck anxiously) I would like to join my husband. Should I go? I miss him so much. What do you say, dear rabbi?

**Baeck**: What could I say? Even though some survived the transports, did I do the right thing? Would it have been better to let everyone know what I knew? To have them put up a fight of resistance to the transports? To go down fighting?

**Woman**: (Anxious, plaintive) Rabbi, please, are you saying I should go? Is there something you're not telling me?

**Baeck**: This memory haunts me. (Tears up)

**Jung**: If you had told people they were going to the gas chambers of Auschwitz and to put up a fight, do you think more people would have been saved?

**Baeck**: I don't know. But did I do the right thing? ...

**Jung**: (After a pause) If you had to do it over again, would you make a different decision?

**Baeck**: Actually, later, at another time, I remember that I did make a different decision. It was in the winter of January 1945. I heard feverish activity coming from the fortifications inside the camp. Deep tunnels were being dug, for storerooms, they said. This did not appear likely. Their real purpose could only have been to serve as gas chambers. We spread the word that if the SS ordered any group to go into these tunnels, they should lie down— simply lie down—wherever they were. There were, perhaps, only 100 guards left at the camp, and it would have taken two of them to carry one of us to a gas chamber.

**Jung:** Maybe this is the answer to your question from the gray zone?

**Baeck:** What are you saying?

**Jung:** That you were in the same situation but didn't keep silent and acted differently. Is not this the essence of "*tsuva*," the Jewish view of repentance, as a returning to the way?

**Baeck:** (Silent in thought, then stands) In April 1945, I was scheduled to be executed. What happened was like something out of a Dostoyevsky novel. I met Adolf Eichmann by chance—he had come to the camp for an inspection. When he saw me, he went pale.

**Woman:** (For Eichmann, in astonishment) Are you still alive?

**Baeck:** You see, a different Rabbi Beck from Moravia had died in the camp, and Eichmann thought it was me. So immediately he issued an order to kill me. I was prepared for this. I gave my wedding rings to my good friend, Jacob, to give to my daughter if he survived. Just then, and at the last possible moment ... the Red Army arrived and liberated the camp!

**Jung:** You were saved ... for a reason!

**Baeck:** Yes. It must be so.

**Jung**: How did you feel when you left the camp for the first time?

**Baeck**: To see a meadow, a wood, a flower, and not to go to bed hungry; to be once again among the living, not the dying—I guess you can imagine the relief and the joy I felt. But then I would remember things. Sometimes a hundred people would die in the camp in a single day, and the day after again, and the day after even more. ... Before me I see their shadows, the shadows of those who died and the shadows of those who led them to their deaths. ... I did not want to leave the camp embittered and with rage for revenge. In that case, they would have won the war after all.

**Jung**: Can you forgive the Germans?

**Baeck**: I, forgive the Germans? Hardly. It is for the Germans to deal with themselves. What happened can never be made good. The German people need to confront the attitudes within themselves that allowed Nazism to flourish. They have to look deeply into their own souls, into their history, their symbols, and their religion. ... Revenge is forbidden to us. It is reserved for God.

Music: Bach, "St. John Passion," #58 Aria, "Es ist vollbracht"

# Scene 7

The stage lights come on brightly. Both men
stand in the strong light. Woman stands between
them.

**Woman:** (To Jung) Say it! Just go ahead and say it!

**Jung:** I have been thinking, Rabbi Baeck. As you were telling
me about your experiences, I felt something happening
in myself. And now there is something I want to say to
you.

**Baeck:** Yes? Go ahead.

**Jung:** As you were speaking, I felt deeply moved, and my
thoughts were in turmoil. Sometimes this happens to me
when I am with a patient in analysis.

**Baeck:** What do you do then?

**Jung:** I wait to see what comes.

**Baeck:** Tell me, then, what came?

**Jung:** Do you know Verdi's "Requiem"?

**Baeck:** Of course. It's one of the great works of sacred music
designed to bring rest to the dead and peace to the living.

**Jung:** In my mind, I heard a section of the part called *Dies Irae*.

**Woman:** (Stridently, as an announcement of doom) "It Is the
Day of Wrath, the Day of Judgment!"

**Jung:** These words came to me: *Quantus tremor est futurus,
Quando Iudex est venturus, Cuncta stricte discussurus.*

**Woman**: (With loud voice, threatening, violent) "How great will be the quaking, when the Judge will come, investigating everything strictly."

**Jung**: Something I learned as a psychologist is that often others know you better than you know yourself. And when the shade of self-deception falls away, you see yourself as you are seen, as you are in that moment.

**Baeck**: What have you seen?

**Woman**: (Looks intensely at Jung) I see a man …

**Jung**: (Continues) … who followed too easily the way of convenience.

**Woman**: I see …

**Jung**: … that I did not consider myself carefully, that I looked the other way and slid too easily from the path of consciousness. In the Bible, it says that on the Day of Judgment we shall see as we are seen. And this is a shattering experience.

**Woman**: I see a man …

**Jung**: … who was seduced by ambition and blinded by fear.

**Baeck**: I do not stand in judgment of you, Professor Jung. It is not mine to judge.

**Jung**: I know that. But the Judge is present as I stand before you naked. I feel it in my bones, and I see myself in another mirror, a mirror of harsh truth without distorting angles of self-deception. (Pause) What I see now is that I fell into a darkness that was invisible to me then.

**Baeck**: (Silently looks at Jung, then nods in acknowledgment) Yes.

**Jung**: I know you can't forgive me. I don't ask for that. But I do hope we can be reconciled, and maybe I can also become reconciled to myself.

**Woman**: (To herself) Can there be reconciliation without forgiveness?

**Jung**: You see, I grew up in a world where the Jew was the "other," a strange and threatening figure of a foreign culture. You could call this anti-Semitism, and it is deeply embedded in Christian and European peoples. I never felt a positive inner connection to anything Jewish. This was changed dramatically in the vision I told you about.

**Baeck**: Yes, I see that now.

**Jung**: I knew no Jews in my childhood and very few in my university years. When I went to Vienna and first met Freud, I admired him but did not feel connected inwardly. He was somehow other. I confess that I did not speak out loudly when his books were being burned in Germany. I was deaf and insensitive, and now I see I was tragically misguided by the habits of collective consciousness. Now I realize: I fell off the path; I went astray. *Ich bin ausgerutscht.*

**Baeck**: (Quietly) But why did you not say something against the Nazis after that early period? Even then you remained silent. Surely you could see what was happening in Germany once Hitler took complete power over the nation.

**Jung**: That is what I mean when I say, *Ich bin ausgerutscht.* I fell off the path.

**Woman**: (To Jung) Now you see why the voice directed you to come to Baeck.

**Baeck**: (After a pause) Dear Professor Jung, you know that Jewish tradition understands that going off the path can be a prelude to returning to the path, even to *tikkun olam*, repairing the world.

**Jung**: (Quietly, in a whisper) *Tikkun olam*?

**Woman**: (With echo effect) *Tikkun olam* ... repairing the world.

Baeck and Jung exit off stage. Woman remains.

Music: Boccherini, "Cello Concerto in B flat Major," Adagio

## Scene 8-A

Jung enters from stage left onto a darkly lit stage.

**Woman**: It's very dark. Can you see the way?

**Jung**: I cannot see the path ahead. The spirits of the dead are here and demand answers. How will I answer them?

**Woman**: You will answer by speaking about the nature of evil and divine darkness.

**Jung**: Yes. That would be a way ahead.

**Woman**: Here is your path. Are you ready to follow it?

**Jung**: (Quietly) I must. You lead the way …

Woman takes Jung's hand, and both exit slowly stage right.

## Scene 8-B

Woman and Baeck enter from stage right.

**Woman**: What will you do now, Rabbi Baeck?
**Baeck**: I will continue my work … restoring the destroyed communities.
**Woman**: And …
**Baeck**: And?
**Woman**: Doing the work of *tikkun olam*?
**Baeck**: Yes, that too.
**Woman**: In the gray zone?
**Baeck**: (After a pause) We all live in the gray zone.

Music: Vivaldi, "Cello Sonata 6," 1st Largo

**End of Play**

# In Retrospect: A Dialogue Between the Authors

**Murray**: My interest in this mysterious meeting between Professor Jung and Rabbi Baeck was sparked when I discovered that nothing much was known about it. I had no idea who Baeck was at the beginning. Why did Jung meet with him? How did this meeting come about? Where and when did they meet? What did they talk about? What happened in the meeting? It was the mystery that fascinated me and that is what you and I have attempted to unveil in the play, to the best of our abilities.

**Henry**: For me as a Jew, the issue of Jung's anti-Semitic remarks was always in the background as his shadow. During my training, my teachers at Yale challenged me, saying: "How can you be a Jungian when you are a Jew." Or "Don't you know he was a Nazi?" Even my teachers in my training as an analyst were very ambivalent and felt much closer to Erich Neumann than to Jung. I dealt with it then by saying: "A great man has a great shadow," and unlike Jungian disciples I did not have a strong personal transference to Jung as a person. But I always felt a need to confront Jung about what he had done.

**Murray**: We chose to open the play with Jung declaring loudly, "But I'm not guilty as charged!" This is a play about the shadow and facing up to it. In your Jungian training in Israel, you were confronted with Jung's shadow right from the start, while in my training in Zurich I never heard about it. For me, this perception came later, and like you I have felt a need to confront Jung with what he said and did. This is what we did in the play. Do you feel satisfied? We do press Jung quite hard in the play with all the accusations that were made against him.

**Henry**: I do and I don't feel satisfied. In the play, when Jung comes to see Baeck at the hotel in Zurich, Baeck does not want to see him. Part of me feels similarly, that I am so angry at Jung, I don't want to speak with him. But another side knows the right thing to do is to let him in and to confront him. I think that many people make a mistake when they do not confront those who have hurt them, who are often unaware of their hurtful behavior. Then the hurt festers, and there is no possibility for reconciliation. Do you feel Baeck is being fair to Jung in the play?

**Murray**: Yes, I think once the conversation gets going, Baeck is able to let Jung say what he needs to say. He even confides in Jung as an analyst! I find this quite astonishing and very touching. But Baeck does not let go of his basic question— "Why did you not speak out even when you knew…?"—and that question still hangs in the air even at the end of the play. In the scene where Jung comes face to face with his shadow and hears Verdi's *Dies Irae* ringing in his ears, Baeck generously reaches out with his words about *tikkun olam*, "repairing the world," and in this gesture he offers Jung a way forward. This is the act of a good rabbi. On the whole, I do think Baeck is fair to Jung but not easy on him. What do you think of Jung's recognition of shadow and his admission of falling off the path? Does this satisfy you as it seems to have satisfied Baeck?

**Henry:** The metaphor of falling off the path is taken from skiing or hiking in the alps, which would be part of Jung's core Swiss identity. It implies that there is a moral track that Jung should have followed, but without noticing, unconsciously, he slipped and went off the track. When Jung meets Baeck, he comes to understand that he was unaware of the process in which he was involved until it was too late. We do know that Jung made private apologies to specific individuals (e.g., James Kirsch and others) but refused to make a public apology. Why he did not make a public apology remains a matter of controversy, but it does count against him. (Similarly, recently there has been a call by some Jungians to make a public apology for the derogatory way Jung refers to "primitives" and "Africans" in his writings.) Overall, I like the image that he lost his moral balance. What do you think of the idea of falling off the track and its implications of shadow enactment? A second question is: Did Jung's shadowy anti-Semitism have a direct or indirect impact on his theories?

**Murray:** I agree that the issue of no public apology remains a sore point. Did Jung really "get it"? I like to think that he did understand his fall off the path of consciousness in some of the statements he made. He must have thought about making a public apology because he was certainly urged by people to do this. So his decision not to take that route must have been based on a judgment that it would do no good but rather worsen the situation. Politically speaking, this may be a correct assessment of the results of public apologies, but from a feeling perspective it seems to fall short. I think Jung was very sensitive to his public image and probably thought that a public display of regret would further tarnish it. We don't see it that way today, of course.

You raise the issue of the relation of cultural attitudes to theory-making and -using. To me, it seems that Jung was trying to eliminate cultural bias and distortion from his theories as much as possible by making cross-cultural comparisons in his theory of archetypes, for instance. From that point of view, every human being is equal and on the same genetic footing, and cultural factors are largely put aside and relativized. Neumann makes this point in a letter to Jung,[2] and as a Jew he was able to use Jung's theories comfortably and found they were of great value in his researches. On the other hand, some people have used Jung's theories in the service of their cultural biases and prejudices. The theory of anima and animus, for instance, can be used to justify sexist views, or it can be used in the opposite direction as Andrew Samuels, for instance, has done. This depends on who is putting the theory to work. In my training and later experience as a teacher and analyst, it never occurred to me that Jung's theory leaned in the direction of anti-Semitism or racism. On the contrary, it has seemed to me that his theories serve to undercut projecting the shadow on to other groups or individuals of differing culture, skin color,

---

[2] Erich Neumann (1934? 2015) *Analytical Psychology in Exile: The Correspondence of C.G. Jung and Erich Neumann*, edited by Martin Liebscher, Princeton, NJ: Princeton University Press, pp.10-15.

or religious affiliation. I think our play shows how this business of retrieving projections works in practice as Jung looks at himself in the mirror and faces up to his shadow. Baeck does the same in his reflections on his decisions taken during the Nazi period. How do you see this?

**Henry**: I think one powerful aspect of the play is that it asks the audience to consider how they might respond emotionally and act in a time of crisis. Baeck exemplifies this self-questioning when he says, "Yes, but did I do the right thing?" as he thinks about decisions he made in the ghetto and the concentration camp, Theresienstadt. Jung, too, feels judged when the image of Verdi's "Requiem" comes to him. As the two men struggle with being judged, the audience must struggle as well, and that gives the play its emotional power. On the other hand, there is danger of armchair morality, of judging others from the comfort of an armchair, without walking 10 miles in their moccasins, to use a Native American metaphor. There is an interesting midrash that asks whether Job was Jewish. The answer is that he was not Jewish because he never doubted himself. By contrast, Baeck is the self-doubter who teaches Jung to doubt himself. From this viewpoint, what do you think of the woman who expresses doubt whether anything can come of the conversation and yet holds together the play of opposites? Also, while Baeck and Jung play themselves throughout the play, the woman plays many roles. What was the inspiration for this dramatic innovation?

**Murray:** I felt the play needed a feminine figure, an anima or soul figure as we say in Jungian discourse. She is the latent eros between the two men. Their previous bond has been ruptured by events, including Jung's comments about Jewish psychology in 1934, but it is still available potentially, presumably now though in the cellar of the unconscious. We call her "Woman" because she does not have a specific identity and does not belong to one man more than to the other. Woman's role is to bring about a situation where the bond can be repaired by bringing the two men together and setting the stage for them to enter into a dialogue. She is their interior voice and feeling – a "still small voice" - sometimes also their memory, and always emotionally tuned in to the situation. In short, she is a kind of shared soul. Her interventions are essential to keep the dynamic movement between the men alive. I like the mystery about her and that the audience is left to wonder who she is and what she is doing here. For me, she adds an essential dimension of depth to the play and makes it a work of depth psychology and not merely a conversation between the two men on the ego level. How do you see her?

**Henry:** Originally, I was skeptical about the role of the woman, which might diminish the direct tension between Jung and Baeck. I also knew that in previous productions of your ensemble, such as the dramatization of scenes from *The Red Book* and the Jung-Neumann correspondence, Dariane Pictet played an important role. Gradually, I understood the advantages of including Woman in the play and also of taking advantage of Dariane's special abilities as an actress. I, too, like the mystery of a woman who cannot be tied down to a specific role and in that way embodies the elusiveness of an anima figure. I like the way that she seems to play the role of both Jung's wife and Baeck's wife in the first scene. She is also the voice who comments on the interaction between the men and gives voice to what Jung is feeling. But I think my favorite scenes with the woman are the two contrasting roles she plays at Theresienstadt. In one scene, she plays an SS officer calling out in rapid fire the names of the arriving Dutch Jews, and it was this experience that inspired Baeck to initiate the now famous cultural life at Theresienstadt. The other poignant scene is based on a real case, that of Dvora Kutchiski, who later became Neumann's closest disciple and one of my supervisors. She asks Baeck whether she should join her husband on the train to the east, and this puts Baeck into a severe moral dilemma. Dvora survived Auschwitz and came to Israel afterward to study with Neumann. The end of the play has the woman playing the role of a guiding anima figure to both Jung and Baeck, and in this way her role at the end of the plays connects with her role at the beginning.

You have talked about the role of the woman in the play and for the audience. What do you think her significance is for Jung and Baeck in the play?

**Murray**: At first she is a goad, like the voice of conscience. She urges both men to meet and to enter into a dialogue. They sense her presence in the atmosphere. She is also memory for both men at different moments. And finally, she is a guide to the future. I think of her as the hidden hand of a guiding presence, the Self. One moment I especially like is when she becomes Jung's experience of the Jewish soul, when he is down with a heart attack in the hospital and she comes to him at night with kosher food. She embodies and shows his connection to the Jewish soul, as we have the men express this connection in their dialogue.

I'd like to discuss the figure of Baeck for a bit. The biographies and testimonials I have read about him make him sound like a Jewish saint. In fact, a rabbi friend of mine, David Freeman, said that this was Baeck's reputation when he studied at the rabbinical seminary in London. However, Hannah Arendt in her book, *Eichmann in Jerusalem*, was very critical of Baeck and said that he cooperated with the Nazis when he should have fought them. At Gershom Scholem's strong objection to this characterization of Baeck, she modulated her tone somewhat but still remained critical. In the play, we have Baeck dealing with the questions she and others have raised about Baeck's role in Berlin and in the camp. What is your view of Baeck after having now thought deeply about this matter and having crafted so much of his language in the play?

**Henry**: Let me begin with Hannah Arendt before considering Baeck. Arendt called Baeck "the Jewish Fuhrer" and accused Baeck and the *Judenrat*, the Jewish Council in the ghettos, of openly collaborating with the Nazis. We do give a hint of that accusation in the play when Baeck reveals his decision to allow Jewish porters to accompany elderly Jews to the transports in Berlin. Although Baeck was doing it out of compassion, some historians and survivors see it as an act of collaboration. At

Theresienstadt, he received somewhat better accommodations as an "elder" although he was never a member of the *Judenrat*. On the other hand, it is important to remember that Hannah Arendt had an ongoing love affair with her teacher and Nazi Party member, Martin Heidegger, both before and after the war. She is said to have tutored him on how to pass the de-Nazification exam, since he never renounced Nazi ideology or condemned the Holocaust.

Gershom Scholem was a close friend of Arendt, but we now know from their correspondence they had a sharp falling out, one in which I believe Baeck would have strongly supported Scholem. Scholem was critical of Arendt's lack of *Ahavat Israel*—love of the Jewish people. Arendt's response says something about her particular form of cosmopolitanism: "I am not moved by any 'love' of this sort, and for two reasons: I have never in my life 'loved' any people or collective—neither the German people, nor the French, nor the American, nor the working class or anything of that sort. I indeed love 'only' my friends and the only kind of love I know of and believe in is the love of persons."[3]

When I think of Baeck, I think of him first and foremost as a Jew who loves the Jewish people. I also think of him as "*yashar.*" This is a Hebrew word that means "upright, straight" in both a physical and a moral sense. He was certainly an intellectual, and his early sermons were called "private conversations with God." Baeck and Jung each contributed

---

[3] Marie Luise Knott (ed.) 2017, *The Correspondence of Hannah Arendt and Gershom Scholem*. Translated by Anthony David. Chicago, IL: University of Chicago Press, p. 206.

chapters to Count Keyserling's *Book of Marriage*. He writes how marriage begins in poetry but is lived out in prose. Baeck was that unique kind of husband who loved only his wife from the beginning of their romance until her death. He was "Prussian" in that he greatly valued order and punctuality. Once a meeting was called for 2:00 p.m. and when no one showed up by 2:01 p.m., he adjourned the meeting and left.

Baeck was a Reform rabbi. It is a remarkable testament to his leadership skills that despite this he was able to guide the entire community of ultraorthodox, orthodox, and secular Jews, something that would be impossible for a Reform rabbi to do today.

Baeck clearly valued Jung's early work. How do you think he would have felt about Jung's later writing, such as *Answer to Job*, *Aion*, the Synchronicity essay, *Memories, Dreams, Reflections*, etc.?

**Murray**: I don't know that Baeck read any of Jung's later writings after he left the camp and was free to study and teach again. He contributed an essay to the Eranos conference in 1947 titled "*Individuum ineffable*," in which he celebrates each person's uniqueness and ultimate value. This would be in line with Jung's notion of individuation as the cardinal principle of psychological development. The theme for that year's conference was "Der Mensch" ("The Human Being"). Interestingly Father Victor White, a close friend and follower of Jung by this time, also gave a lecture at that conference. His was titled "*Anthropologia rationalis* (The Aristotelian-Thomist Conception of Man)." Jung attended the conference but did not lecture that year due to illness. This was also Erich Neumann's introduction to the Eranos gathering, and from here on until the end of his life in 1960 he was a regular lecturer and was generally considered to be the most brilliant of Jung's pupils. So Baeck was in a pretty tight Jungian circle when he gave this lecture—his one and only Eranos lecture. How he responded to this situation and to what he heard around him we don't know, except that a photograph was taken of the two men sitting at the famous round table, which shows them in a very congenial and friendly engagement with one another [see photo on the cover]. This is an important piece of evidence that a reconciliation of importance took place during their meeting at the Savoy Hotel in Zurich a year earlier.

I rather doubt that Baeck read Jung's later work because he was so preoccupied with his own mission of restoring the Jewish communities in Europe and with teaching and writing. His last major work, published in German in 1955, was titled *Dieses Volk: Jüdische Existenz* (translated as *This People Israel: The Meaning of Jewish Existence* and published in English in 1964). In the preface he writes these moving lines:

> This book was written during dark times. In the days when the annihilation of Jewish life had been announced and was being actively pursued, the writer felt impelled to render an account of this Jewish life, this Jewish people.
>
> The first chapters of this book were written in the writer's old house; those following were written in the concentration camp, on any scrap of paper that came to hand, whenever a quiet hour was to be found. When the liberation came and the war ended, the bundle of pages which

had been hidden repeatedly had become a very personal possession. By itself it told of the miracle of survival.

But the events have become history, and the experiences of that time have been transmuted into spirit. The present called and asked, and all the days were to answer. It thus seemed that, after all, this book should speak before men and bear witness. May it then make its way to them.[4]

I think Baeck would have appreciated Jung's *Answer to Job* as a personal statement of his attempt to come to terms with the problem of evil. Certainly, Jung's solution to the problem would not have been Baeck's, as it also wasn't Victor White's.

Henry, you and I lectured on Neumann's and Jung's struggles with the problem of evil at the Jung-Neumann conference in Tel Aviv in 2015.[5] You based your comments on Neumann's work, *Depth Psychology and a New Ethic*, which was published in 1949. Jung wrote an appreciative Foreword to the book indicating his approval, which was a surprise to some of his Zurich students, as you know. What do you think Baeck would have made of Neumann's work? We touch on the theme of "the gray zone" in the play. Isn't this also what Neumann was writing about?

---

[4] Leo Baeck, 1965. *This People Israel: The Meaning of Jewish Existence*. Translated by Albert H. Friedlander. London: W.H. Allen, p. 3

[5] Henry Abramovitch, "The Search for a New Ethic: Professional and Clinical Dilemmas"; Murray Stein, "Erich Neumann and C.G. Jung on 'The Problem of Evil,'" in Erel Shalit & Murray Stein (eds.), 2016, *Turbulent Times, Creative Minds: Erich Neumann and C.G. Jung in Relationship* (1933-1960). Asheville, NC: Chiron Publications, pp. 165-196.

**Henry**: Neumann understood the evolution of ethical awareness in terms of three stages: primal unity, the old ethic and the
new ethic. The first stage of "primal unity" parallels the primal
unity of mother and infant. In this stage, the group is responsible for every individual, and each individual is viewed as
the incarnation of the whole group. What is paramount is
loyalty to the group, and not right-and-wrong. Baeck would
understand these feelings as part of "*ahavat* Israel," the love of
the Jewish people in which each Jew is responsible for all others.

The old ethic is familiar from the Ten Commandments:
"Thou shalt not kill! Thou shalt not steal!" Its archetypal image
is that of the wise, devout, spiritual hero acting as a person with
immense self-control. The old ethic does lead to a strengthening
of the ego over the tyranny of the unconscious but heightens
the conscious/unconscious split. Indeed, it was the failure of the
old ethic during the Holocaust that pushed Neumann to write
his first masterwork, *Depth Psychology and the New Ethic*. But
Jung argued convincingly that ethics are relative, depending on
one's point of view. Jung wrote in a letter to Dr. Fierz in 1949:
"It is an actual fact that what is good to one appears evil to the
other."[6] Moral life under the old ethic becomes an endless
struggle between our good and bad parts, representing the dual
and dueling aspects of the human soul. In Jungian terms, one
might say that the ego over-identifies with the collective values
of society and so denies the shadow. Neumann showed how
easily the idealism of the old ethics leads to atrocities. Baeck as

---

[6] C.G. Jung, 1973, *Letters*, Vol. 1. Edited by Gerhard Adler. Princeton, NJ: Princeton
University Press, p. 519.

a rabbi was steeped in the tradition of the old ethic of the Ten Commandments, but he would understand the hubris of trying to be too good.

The core of the new ethic is to be conscious of evil and take to responsibility for the dark side. Our fascination with profound evil in art and literature, from Raskolnikov in Dostoevsky's *Crime and Punishment* to Iago in Shakespeare's *Othello*, from serial killers to vampire movies, reflects our secret desire to know this hidden, evil side. Knowing our evil side can prevent the murderous unconscious projections associated with the old ethic. I think Baeck would be skeptical of Neumann's new ethic since it emphasizes consciousness over being a "*Mensch*," a decent human being. However, I do think that Baeck would understand the gray zones between primary unity of being part of "this people Israel" in which each Jew is a guarantor for every other Jew, the old ethic of always striving to do the right thing even though it may involve suppression and repression, and the importance of taking responsibility for one's evil urge as required in the new ethic and Hassidism. Baeck certainly understood the gray zone (the term comes from another survivor, Primo Levi), as we show in the play.

Martin Buber, in *Eclipse of God*, made a penetrating critique of Jung (and implicitly Neumann). Buber asked, in the wake of the rise of Hitler: "When one hears that inner voice, how can one tell whether it is the voice of the Self or the Devil?"[7]

---

[7] Martin Buber, 1988. *Eclipse of God: Studies in the Relation between Religion and Philosophy*. Translated by Maurice Friedman, Atlantic Highlands, NJ: International Humanities Press, pp. 33-4.

How do you think Jung would respond? What do you think of those remarkable visions Jung had in hospital in 1944?

**Murray**: Jung was not naïve about the voice of the Self. He held that the Self has a dark side and can lead one astray ethically. He compared it to the alchemical Mercurius, a very tricky character indeed. So he would agree with Buber that consciousness must be prepared to test the "voice" and not simply to trust and obey.

Concerning visions, as we know Jung was given to having them from time to time in his life, but this set of visions was special. They occurred while he was under medical treatment after his heart attack. He describes them in *Memories, Dreams, Reflections* and says they were "the most tremendous things I have ever experienced."[8] In the play, we have Baeck suggest that perhaps these visions brought him into contact with the Jewish soul. They certainly connected him to a deep layer in his unconscious where he was one with the Jewish mystic, Rabbi Simon ben Jochai, who by tradition was the visionary creator of Kabbalah. Jung had been studying Cabalistic writings and authors, which we can see from his book *Psychology and Alchemy* published in 1944, and he would refer often to the Jewish mystical writings in his later works, especially in *Aion, Answer to Job* and *Mysterium Coniunctionis*. I think these visions took him to a spiritual level where he could transcend his conventional prejudices and collective attitudes, but that would still take a good deal of work on a practical level. This is what

---

[8] C.G. Jung, 1961. *Memories, Dreams, Reflections*, New York: Vintage, p. 295.

the play is about: the work of facing up to the shadow and moving into a new, enlarged consciousness that "gets it" on the behavioral level. At the end of the play, Baeck shows a way forward with his reference to the notion of *tikkun olam*. Do you see Jung in his last years as a person effectively engaged in this project?

**Henry:** I do. I can see it in how photographs of Jung changed over time. As a young man, he seems fierce, uptight, and judgmental. In his later years, he looks serene yet playful, a smiling wise old man who does not take himself too seriously. I also believe there is an element of *tikkun olam* in his process of individuation. Individuation, which means knowing yourself more and more, always involves confronting the shadow. The individual's work with the shadow also detoxifies the collective shadow, as illustrated in the Cabalistic doctrine that the holiest sparks can only be found and redeemed in the dark side. Similarly, *Memories, Dreams, Reflections* not only showed Jung's remarkable personal journey, but reading it made it possible for me and many others to feel that we, too, might be able to set out on a journey. Even in his late book on flying saucers one can sense his search for the Self in unexpected places. Jung was also a replacement child, born after three previous newborns had died in which his mother's unresolved grief was folded into his psyche. His psyche may have been centered on an absence: the dead siblings he never knew. Jung hints at the intensity of his experience as a replacement child in *The Red Book*.[9] His

---

[9] C.G. Jung, 2009. *The Red Book: Liber Novus*. Edited by Sonu Shamdasani. New

lifelong ambition and impressive creativity may have been a way to prove himself worthy and unique in his own right, resolving for all what he could not resolve for himself.

Let's think about some of the turning points in the play. Jung comes to Baeck's hotel because of his dreams. But why do you think Baeck opens the door to him? Why does Baeck feel that he can tell Jung about his experiences at Theresienstadt and the gray zone? How does the association to Verdi's *Requiem* come to Jung?

**Murray**: We don't know for sure what drove Jung to force this encounter with Baeck, but the motivation must have been quite urgent because he did insist on seeing Baeck when he came to Zurich in October 1946. My guess is that he felt an inner demand like the one we dramatize in the play when he speaks of the Voice demanding that he go and see Baeck. But it takes him a while to discover what his motive for this visit really is. At first, it is just to explain himself, to offer a defense, and to clear his name with a Jewish authority. Later, he discovers deeper reasons. He needs to make a confession. And Baeck, when pressed, could not say "no" to Jung when he was at his hotel room door. Perhaps this was out of politeness or a sense of human decency, a kind of ethical attitude. Baeck was a *Mensch*, as you describe it. I suspect this was it. And then the encounter—tense, conflicted, ambiguous. And the miracle is that they enter into what Buber would call an I-Thou dialogue. They open up to each other, step by step. They share deeply their

York: W.W. Norton & Company, p. 296.

struggles and subjective experiences. This is not just polite conversation. It is profound exchange, human to human. And from this genuine dialogue, Jung begins to see himself in another dimension. He looks in a mirror and sees himself as others, like Baeck for instance, have seen him, and this is a shock to him. This is what happens in genuine dialogue, don't you think? One sees oneself from the other's point of view. And then, suddenly, Jung's inner ear detects Verdi's gripping Requiem music and the chilling words from *Dies Irae*—"It is the day of wrath, the day of Judgment." Jung now stands naked before the Judge, not Baeck but the Almighty as He is depicted in the Book of Revelation. Jung was steeped in the Bible, and this would have been a familiar association.

But back to you: Why did Baeck open the door, and more than the door, why did he open his heart to Jung?

**Henry**: There is a fascinating discussion in the Talmud concerning how many times a person should ask for forgiveness from a person he or she has offended. One rabbi says one should ask once but really mean it. A second rabbi claims that one should keep asking until the sinned-against person literally throws you out of their house. The mainstream Jewish tradition, however, adopted a middle way of asking three times. To ask more might lead the person to become enraged and so bring sin on himself. Fewer than three times might make the person feel that the repentance was not sincere. Asking for forgiveness three times is ongoing Jewish practice, especially before Yom Kippur, the Day of Atonement, and one that Baeck certainly would have been familiar with. In the play, we subtly incorporate this Jewish tradition when the woman encourages Jung to knock for a third time and adds that if he won't answer now, he never will.

I agree that Baeck may have responded out of a sense of decency. But it may have also related to the history of anti-Semitism and the Holocaust. Jews over the centuries under persecution have often knocked on the doors of their neighbors but with very mixed results. During the Holocaust, people who did open their doors and their hearts, thus saving Jews, are called "righteous gentiles," and a tree is planted in their honor at Yad Vashem in Jerusalem. I think, in the end, Baeck did not want to be a person who closed his door and his heart to a man in distress. It is also possible that Baeck knew that Jung had operated as a spy for the OSS (the predecessor to the CIA). He was called "Agent 488," and his handler, Allen W. Dulles, later remarked: "Nobody will probably ever know how much Prof Jung contributed to the allied cause during the war."[10]

Once the door is opened, Baeck, however, is ambivalent and does not allow Jung to discuss "niceties" but gets right down to business. What do you make of Jung's initial reaction? Later, both Baeck and Jung discuss their images of the Jews and the Germans, and how they are interrelated. What do you make of this?

**Murray**: I thought this was a fascinating part of their conversation. It is the basis of dialogue, to get to this level and exchange what are usually carefully hidden thoughts and

---

[10] Deidre Bair, 2004. *Jung: A Biography*. New York: Little, Brown, p.492.

feelings about each other. How often does this happen? For instance, in analysis this conversation may take place, but in normal social intercourse it does not. I remember Paul Mendes-Flohr saying that dialogue is possible only when both parties disclose their feelings and views, listen to the other, and are able to discuss differences. This does not mean they will agree in the end, but without this level of trust and openness no movement is possible. Jung and Baeck reach this level in the play, and this makes possible a turn in their relationship. What we have shown in this play is a dialogue emerging and developing and bringing about a transformation. With Jung and Baeck, this takes place on an individual level. Do you think this can take place on a collective level? For instance, in my country, the United States, the intractable issue is entrenched racism, the African and the European populations coming to terms with one another. So far, this has not been very successful despite many efforts. I know that in your country, Israel, you have been individually engaged in dialogue between Jews and Palestinians. Has there been any headway on a societal level that you can see? Maybe our play can offer some guidance. I don't know. What do you think?

**Henry**: Life is lived in the tension between our individual identities and our collective identities. I am both myself and a Jew, just as you are yourself as well as an American living in Switzerland. We both identify ourselves as Jungian analysts. The difficulty arises when someone else perceives or "forces" me into my collective identity alone, as when they may say, "You Jews" or "You Americans are always …" In Israel/Palestine, there is a strong tendency to project the collective shadow onto the "Other," especially when the contact is not personal but only via violence and the media. This tendency to demonize the other in their collective identity makes me very pessimistic about the possibility of peace and reconciliation. On the individual level, in contrast, there are many examples of personal encounter and dialogue that exist outside the confines of the collective. One of my very best friends, Raja Shehadeh, is a Palestinian who wrote a book about our friendship called *Where the Line is Drawn.*[11] He discusses in an exquisite way the tension between our personal friendship and the collective enmity in which it is situated and when he felt he needed to break off our relationship. Subsequently, he felt able to resume our unique friendship, and we have remained close friends ever since. A somewhat similar dynamic occurred between Baeck and Jung, who had been together at The School of Wisdom in 1920s. In the play, Jung and Baeck play out their tension between the personal relation they had and their collective identity as "Nazi sympathizer" and "Jew," and they are able to reconcile. The photo on the cover of this book of the two of them at the Eranos Conference shows how much they are engaged with one another. I do think the play gives hope by showing that honest, open-hearted dialogue can lead to reconciliation. That would be my hope for the Middle East.

---

[11] Raja Shehadeh, 2017. *Where the Line is Drawn: Crossing Boundaries in Occupied Palestine.* London: Profile Books.

We have discussed the opening of the play. What do you think of the two endings, one for Jung, one for Baeck, and the woman in both?

**Murray**: We spent a lot time, you and I, discussing the last scenes, which are very short and show Jung and Baeck both facing an unknown and uncertain future. Both men lived on, Baeck for another 10 years, Jung for another 15, and both remained very productive in their old age. Baeck traveled, taught in the United States, England and Israel, and finished his book, *This People Israel*, begun in the 1930s in Germany and worked on while he was in Theresienstadt in bits and pieces. Jung wrote works that would become classics in his oeuvre, "The Psychology of the Transference," *Aion*, *Answer to Job*, "Synchronicity: An Acausal Connecting Principle," and *Mysterium Coniunctionis*. In this last scene of the play, we see Jung looking for a way ahead and Woman suggesting that he write about the problem of evil and Divine Darkness, which he did five years later in *Answer to Job*. I see these late works as Jung's contributions to *tikkun olam*, attempts at repairing the world and healing our collective psychic splits. They are also his answer to the millions of dead in the war and the Holocaust. Baeck recognizes that we all live in the gray zone and that the great ethical issues we face have no simple solutions. Our choices are made in the gray zone where we are not sure, where we have doubts, but where we nevertheless have to take decisions. I hope people take this message home with them from the play: It is not an easy thing to be responsible, but we must do our best while knowing that moral perfection is not possible. Is this how you see the outcome of this dialogue between the analyst and the rabbi?

**Henry**: Both Jung and Baeck were transformed by their encounter. Each one can no longer continue in the life path in which they had previously traveled but must enter the dark and gray zone, without knowing where they are going. For me, the ending highlights the role of Woman as an anima and spirit guide for both Jung and Baeck. She is the one who points the way to Jung and his task of confronting evil. Likewise, she helps Baeck see that his task of restoring the destroyed Jewish communities of Europe must be carried out in the gray zone and as part of *tikkun olam*. Listening to that guiding inner voice allows one to find the place for which one is intended, yet does not know how to reach. The play begins with opening a door and ends with two journeys toward *tikkun olam*.

**Murray**: It has been a pleasure to work with you on this play, Henry. I don't have a biological brother, but now I have the feeling that must come with such a fraternal relationship. You have written a perceptive book on this topic, *Brothers and Sisters: Myth and Reality*, your Fay Lectures in 2014. Writing this play with you has brought a fantasy of brotherhood into the realm of reality for me.

# Reflections
# by the Cast

# From the Perspective of an Actor in the Play

## By Paul Brutsche

I view the play from the perspective of "C.G. Jung," whose role I enacted in the performances of the play. Because Jung's attitude changes very much from the beginning to the end of the play, showing this evolution within a 90-minute performance is a special acting challenge. It is this transformation that brings the play to life and makes it a convincing piece of theater.

At the beginning, Professor Jung takes the initiative to bring about an encounter with Rabbi Baeck. Convinced of his innocence, he wants to defend himself against unjustified accusations and malicious insinuations. This is a self-assured Jung who finds himself confronted with nefarious accusations from his enemies and who actively seeks to restore his reputation, to "explain himself" and to justify his position. He presents himself as the victim of evil strategies.

In his effort to correct these unjustified accusations, he overlooks other, subtler forms of questionable behavior. At first, when confronted by Baeck, he does not want to admit that he accepted the presidency of the International Medical Psychotherapy Association not only for ethical reasons but also due to certain shadowy advantages. With the presidency, he and his psychology were guaranteed a favored position in Germany at the expense of Freudian psychoanalysis. Jung is forced to admit to Baeck that there were not only honorable intentions but also questionable shadow motives in his decision to accept the role.

Jung then finds himself confronted by Baeck with two accusations: The first is that in writing about "Jewish psychology" in 1934 he said that Jews had never produced a cultural form of their own but had always fed off of host cultures ("the Jew as cultural parasite" allegation), and the second is that he had not spoken out publicly against the great evil that had appeared in the form of National Socialism. These accusations charge him with a lack of understanding "Jewish psychology" on the one hand and with a lack of civil courage and empathy on the other. Baeck says pointedly: "You looked the other way!" Jung leaves these accusations practically unchallenged in the play, thus indicating that a process of self-questioning has begun in him.

Under the pressure of Baeck's dramatic depictions of evil that he had been exposed to in Theresienstadt, Jung experiences an emotional reversal. He begins to grasp the horror of the times in all its inscrutability and malice. He is no longer able to stay detached from it, to remain intellectually uninvolved and to look "in the other direction." He is forced to face evil directly. Dodging evil, ignoring its reality, and intellectually relativizing and looking away from its physically real immediacy are no longer an option.

In a further step, Jung recognizes the fact that the Jewish people had always seemed unfamiliar to him, as being different and strange. This was in accordance with a collective, culturally conditioned attitude. Here, a decisive change in his consciousness occurs. This is mediated by the memory of a vision in which he had experienced himself as a participant in a mystical Cabalistic wedding where he assumed the identity of an ancient Jewish sage, Simon ben Jochai. Instead of feeling alienated from things Jewish, he experiences an overwhelming spiritual closeness. Significantly, this transformational vision was initiated by a physical boundary experience in a hospital where Jung was recovering from a broken leg that almost led to his death due to unexpected complications. This physical slipping on the ice in the street echoes the moral "slipping off the path" that he confesses to Baeck in the poignant words, "*Ich bin ausgerutscht*" ("I fell off the path"). The accident led him to an opening and expansion of consciousness, as is often the case with critical experiences of loss of power and control.

In the end, Jung acknowledges his guilt. His deep and honest insight goes beyond a superficial admission and recognition of his questionable behavior. It is a profound insight carried further by a religious consciousness and leading to repentance. Reference is made here to Verdi's "Requiem" when he hears in his inner world the music of the passage, Dies irae, and remembers the Latin verse: *Quantus tremor est futurus, cuando judex est venturus, cuncta stricte discussurus* ("how great will be the quaking, when the Judge will come, investigating everything strictly"), and he recalls a scene from the Book of Revelation ("In the Bible it says that on the Day of Judgment we shall see as we are seen. And this is a shattering experience."). This introduces a dimension of coming to terms with one's own shadow in a realm beyond the boundaries of ego-consciousness, which are transgressed, and where one no longer stands in judgment before a human counterpart but before a transcendent Judge.

In summary, the play shows us an encounter with the shadow in several stages and dimensions. At the start, there is denial and self-righteous defense against malicious insinuations in the name of self-interest and for the preservation of the persona. This gives way to the analytical recognition of unconscious shadow motives. Upon this follows the moral awareness of a devaluing and indifferent attitude toward the "other's" thinking and being, accompanied by the emotional shock of realizing the extent of the injustice suffered by the "other." Then comes the recognition of the objective and active reality of evil. Through the visionary experience, a decisive turning point is reached: It brings an experience of intimate closeness to the rejected "other" and the overwhelming mystical union that creates a lasting bond. This is symbolically expressed in the image of the sacred marriage of Malchuth to Tifereth. Finally, there is the religious consciousness of one's deep existential dubiousness as a person.

In the course of this process of becoming conscious, the true meaning of Jung's initiation of a conversation with Rabbi Baeck is revealed. If initially it was for the purpose of self-defensive explanation and self-justification toward his Jewish friends and enemies, it turns out ultimately to be about making conscious a deep spiritual connection with the "Jewish soul."

At the very end of the play, the theme of evil opens to another dimension: the question of evil as such, or "absolute evil" as Jung would speak of it. Jung recognizes that his own insecurities, misconduct, and dubiousness and his confrontation with objective evil pose the fundamental question of the nature of evil and the dark mystery of evil in God.

The play shows universally valid dimensions of dealing with the personal shadow and suprapersonal evil. As in Greek tragedy, it has a liberating effect. Beyond that, it is thought-provoking in that it takes us into the paradoxical and mysterious depths of the problem of evil. Evil is a mystery. This is expressed during the last scene with Jung. On a darkened stage, he realizes that the spirits of the dead must be answered. The question of evil has not been satisfactorily answered in Christianity, which has projected evil onto a devil. In order to find an answer, Jung lets himself be led by an anima figure:

**Woman**: Here is your path. Are you ready to follow it?

**Jung**: I must. You lead the way.

The answer must come from the depths of the unconscious and its healing and orienting images, i.e. from the soul's intuition, which reaches beyond the narrow horizon of a limited ego-reflection.

# Breaking the Silence

### By John Hill

Rabbi Leo Baeck was a great scholar, a man of the heart, and a leader of his people. During the war, he was interned in Theresienstadt for three years. There he learned about the fate of fellow Jews who were sent to the East. They were to end up in the gas chambers of Auschwitz. Later he was criticized for remaining silent. To speak or not to speak: that was Baeck's dilemma. His answer: "No one should know. If the Council of Elders were informed, the whole camp would know within a few hours. Living in the expectation of death by gassing would only be the harder. And this death was not certain for all."[12] For Baeck, destroying hope would be worse than death in the gas chambers.

Citing passages from the Kabbalah, Ernst Bloch in his monumental work, *The Principle of Hope,* draws attention to the intrinsic connection between hope and imprisonment in Jewish tradition. According to the Kabbalah, God created several worlds but destroyed them because they were without the human being. Isaac Luria's Cabbalistic notion of God's contraction (*tsimtsum*) at the beginning of creation implies that God goes into exile and captivity with humanity. The motif repeats itself again and again in Jewish history: the captivity in Egypt, Babylon, and Nazi Germany. I quote: "Exile lent the *Deus*

---

[12] Baker Leonard, *Days of Sorrow and Pain*. London & New York: Macmillan Publishing, 1978, p. 311.

*Spes* (God of hope) the most painful radiance because Jahweh himself, together with his people, seemed to have gone into exile. God as '*Shechina*,' i.e. as the presence of his light, is now, according to the Cabbala, himself homeless in a creation in which man does occur but is imprisoned: the *Shechina* shines not from the beginning of the world but as a messianic light of consolation and hope."[13] Bloch's *The Principle of Hope* was written at the same time that Baeck had to live and uphold that virtue while imprisoned in the confines of Theresienstadt.

Baeck shone as a man of indomitable hope. Night after night, he organized a series of lectures in the camp. Various Jewish speakers spoke on the works of Plato, Kant, Spinoza, Maimonides and others. Baeck lectured on Ancient Greece. Despite being conquered by more powerful neighbors, Greek culture survived thousands of years. Baeck did not advocate open rebellion, but his lectures expressed a subtle note of defiance against the Nazi persecutors. Baeck gave many examples of how in the end truth overcomes might. I quote his biographer, Leonard Baker: "In Judaism to hope is a duty, and Baeck's lectures gave those people reason to fulfil that duty."[14]

For me personally, it has been a privilege to get to know this saintly man. He stands out as a man of indomitable faith, hope, and love. He is an example for us all to remain truthful to our inner core values, especially when facing a hostile environment that threatens those values. Leo Baeck's words and

---

[13] Bloch, Ernst, *The Principle of Hope* volume 3. Boston: MIT Press Paperback 1996 [written 1938-1947], p. 1236.
[14] Bloch, Ernst, *The Principle of Hope* volume 3. Boston: MIT Press Paperback 1996 [written 1938-1947], p. 1236.

life tell us not to be afraid, but to remain courageous and defiant knowing that one day truth will be victorious. Alive or dead, we are asked to bequeath a legacy that admonishes us not to surrender to those forces that attempt to extinguish the very nature of what it means to be human.

Keeping Baeck's biography in mind, I gratefully accepted the role I was assigned as antagonist to C.G. Jung in Murray Stein's and Henry Abramovitch's *The Analyst and the Rabbi*. We cannot know if the figure of "Rabbi Baeck" in the play corresponds exactly with the historical Rabbi Baeck. It is, however, a narrative about transformation. In this play "Baeck" and "Jung," the performers and the spectators have the opportunity to re-live those dark times and ask themselves what they would have done, and what they could have done. There is no simple answer. We are asked to immerse ourselves in the story and, hopefully, break the silence of the heart to speak our own truth. It is imperative that we learn to do so in a culture that celebrates fake news.

Let me now outline some of the dramatic moments in the Baeck/Jung encounter that highlight the conflict between these extraordinary men. In the initial Scene, 1 (as Rabbi Baeck) don't want to meet Jung. Jung is insistent. He knocks on my hotel door three times. I have to let him in, but I remain stiff, distant, and reserved. In Scene 2, I cannot hold back my emotions any longer and I make a full attack on Jung. I cannot understand how he could remain silent when the Nazis were exterminating not only Jews but also psychiatric patients. In Scene 3, I am incensed that Jung claimed Jews do not have a culture of our own but live only from the culture of others. Jung's understanding of "Jewish psychology" falls far short of the deep, authentic, and creative contribution that Jews have made to German culture. I remind Jung of the tens of thousands who died while fighting for "*das Vaterland*" in World War I. How could Jung see us as mere parasites? This sounds like something straight out of Nazi propaganda. Toward the end of the scene, emotions are high. I will not let Jung off lightly. I succeed in making a dent in his defenses when I describe how Jews were hunted down, robbed, murdered, and terrorized. Jung becomes aware of the consequences of his silence.

In Scene 4, Jung's heart begins to soften when I tell him about the ordeals I underwent in Theresienstadt. Like a horse, I was hitched to a wagon that carried garbage and dead bodies through the streets every morning. I lament the death of my five sisters and of the thousands who died with them. In Scene 6, my suffering and the suffering of my people awaken Jewish affinities lodged deep in Jung's soul. A heart connection emerges. It is then that I am able to confide in Jung the terrible conflict I had to endure in remaining silent, knowing that my fellow Jews were being sent to the Auschwitz gas chambers. Reconciliation comes in the final scene when both of us, caught up in remembering one of the darkest moments of human history, appreciate the meaning of life in a gray zone. Both of us are torn as we endure the trials of confronting good and evil, uncertain if evil is good or good is evil. Jung finally admits he fell off the path, and I remind him that in Jewish tradition falling off the path can be a prelude to returning to the path, even to *tikun olam*, repairing the world, which could also be understood as a redemption of all that *tsimtsum* entailed.

At this stage of the performance I felt a strong urge to express some kind of physical gesture of reconciliation. In a dignified way that would have been in keeping with Baeck's character, I approach Jung and put my hand on his shoulder.

In enacting the role of "Baeck," I cherished the signifi-cance of Leo Baeck not only as a man of deep love but one who could vent his anger when confronted with denial. The role was difficult. It was very emotional and dramatic. I had to constantly enact a palette of different emotions, switching quickly from being cold and dismissive to being angry and filled with rage, then to feeling sadness, guilt, and finally arriving at compassion. On several occasions, I had to chant prayers and cite biblical passages. In the rehearsals when praying the ancient Kaddish for the dead, I got so immersed in the Baeck's soulful lamentations that the next lines entirely escaped my mind. Luckily, this did not happen in the performances.

It was hard at times to keep attacking my friend and colleague, Paul Brutsche, who was acting as Jung. I already had to do so in other performances, playing the roles of Victor White and Erich Neumann in performances of their cor-respondences with Jung, and Elijah, Izdubar and Philemon from *The Red Book*. Dramatic confrontations onstage seem to be our fate, but our friendship has held. The role of the myste-rious woman in the play, performed by Dariane Pictet, was crucial for keeping focus on the core conflict between Jung and Baeck. Her powerful temperament prevented a pattern of avoidance. Mirroring a reconciling symbol, she inspired the two men to be more related and truthful with each other. Finally, the music of Barbara Miller's cello performance, some of which came from the original music of Theresienstadt, captured the deep emotions of those times and had a transformative effect on all who witnessed a soul-searching performance.

I believe this imaginative and dramatic rendering of a historical encounter can have a transformative effect on the future of Jungian Psychology. Although the play is well-researched, it goes far beyond the actual events that happened between Baeck and Jung at Zürich's Savoy Hotel Baur en Ville in October 1946. It is a message of hope, a virtue deeply rooted in Jewish tradition. In witnessing the huge struggle between analyst and rabbi, performers and indeed spectators were moved in such ways that they could appreciate human shortcomings through the lenses of the heart. D.H. Lawrence, in his essay "Why the Novel Matters," wrote that a well-written novel is like a cardiograph of a life that is lived or, inversely, it sensitizes us to the deadness of inauthentic existence.[15] I believe this play succeeds in breaking the silence of denial and sensitizing our hearts to the men and women who are faced with terrible choices in dark times of confusion and turmoil. Even if Jung did not apologize publicly for his statements on Jewish psychology in the 1930s, and we cannot do it for him, we can, nevertheless, learn from the errors of those of high repute so that they do not get repeated in the future. Jung once wrote: "One does not become enlightened by imagining figures of light, but by making the darkness conscious."[16] In breaking the silence of the heart, I appreciate this play as an invitation to open our hearts to witness from yet another perspective the "lingering shadows" of the past.[17]

---

[15] Lawrence, D. H. (1936) "Why the Novel Matters," in *Phoenix: The Posthumous Papers of D. H. Lawrence*, Edward D. McDonald, ed., New York, Viking Press, 1968, pp. 533-538.

[16] Jung, C.G., *Collected Works*, 13, §335.

[17] Maidenbaum, A, & Martin, S. (eds.) *Lingering Shadows: Jungians, Freudians and*

# Reflections on the Role of Woman in "The Analyst and the Rabbi"

**By Dariane Pictet**

The play invites us into the inner world of two persons, both known for their remarkable achievements who yet are also, as giants often are, criticized and misunderstood. Rabbi Baeck was a towering figure in Germany and beyond, and Jung's psychology was a beacon in a world of scientific materialism and the emphasis on outer concerns. We watch them struggle with each other, delve into their souls, and question themselves to get to a healing truth. Simultaneously, we, too, are drawn into our own darkness and strengthened in our desire for wholeness.

"The Analyst and the Rabbi" shows us two exceptional men who have the courage and the honesty to reflect on their past actions and share with each other particularly difficult decisions at key moments of their lives. At first, we may turn from one to the other wanting answers, something black or white that could fit with our need for structure and clarity, We might feel self-righteous in our demands for accountability, but the play takes us down the corridors of hidden motivations and intentions. We are drawn into the meanderings of psyche where light is scarce, where our humanity falters, and, if we are courageous enough, we might ask ourselves difficult questions, avoided questions. Could we have done, said, or even thought

*Anti-Semitism*. Boston & London, Shambhala, 1991.

things that would be too horrendous to reveal to a stranger, a respected but unknown colleague? This is precisely what the play has Jung and Baeck do in a Zürich hotel room in 1946, facilitated by an inner faculty called Woman.

Unlike Jung or Baeck, Woman seemed at first to lack definition, and only a character of equal strength could find her place in this intimate piece, yet it is this very fluidity of being that gives her cohesion. She is there without being there, invisible to them, yet powerful in her inner presence. Woman embodies an invisible archetypal realm, beyond judgment, present and attuned to the action but without a personal identity. At times she feels drawn to a particular emotional energy field and speaks or acts for the character from there, humanizing herself briefly and returning to a witnessing attitude.

She functions as a Greek chorus, expressing what the characters have hidden or could not express and encouraging them to open their hearts. She becomes Baeck's living memory in his poignant evocation of the woman in the camp who wants advice about joining her husband in Auschwitz. Has he done "the right thing" in not divulging where such a journey would end? She doesn't say but enacts his tormented recollection of the concentration camp, gives flesh to the infamous Rahm who cold-bloodedly sends Mrs. Zucker to the death camp on the pretense that she will soon lie in her husband's arms. Woman amplifies Baeck's remembrance of the daily struggles for survival in Theresienstadt, and the moments of relief that permitted prisoners to endure. Woman echoes the many responsibilities Baeck shouldered as best he could. And she also carries tribal, collective memory, reading the names of the dead, the forsaken, to bring healing to those who remember and grieve. If Woman represents soul, it is in its Anima Mundi aspect, tempered by an awareness that reaches beyond the human frame and is softened by love and forgiveness.

Yet, she is firm. She doesn't try to sway the public with information that could divert her implacable sense of justice. She doesn't inform the audience that Jung was a staunch defender of the Jewish cause during the war, as related by the American OSS officer Alan Dulles. She doesn't give voice to Baeck's critics, such as Hannah Arendt, that he collaborated with the SS in the division of labor in the camps. Rather, she persuades Jung to share his mystical experience of his connection with the "Jewish soul." She embodies the Jewish nurse who fed him when he was in the hospital, helping him to find a feeling connection and to articulate his oneness with those he claims he didn't know. Jung's confession reveals his humanity and inspires Baeck to share his own troubled conscience.

Woman's role punctuates the drama's movement toward completion. She begins by encouraging Jung to meet with Baeck, and vice versa, reassuring them and coaxing them to move beyond their ambivalence or resentment, drawn to one man then the other without preference or conflict. Moving between the phenomenal world and the deeply intimate, Woman gives body to their inner life, the turmoil and dilemmas, anxieties, and fears. At the play's climax, she embodies the cold voice of self-judgment of Jung's *Dies Irae*: the punitive, self-condemning voice of a conscience without peace. This prompts Baeck's compassionate articulation of the Jewish idea of conversion, T'shuva, of transformation through atonement. She asks reflectively if there can "be reconciliation without forgiveness," pointing him toward a self-forgiveness that could dissolve the inner conflict preventing at-one-ness, the return to an undivided, unblemished relationship with oneself and the world. This returning to the light is *tikkun olam*, where our actions, born out of compassion, can be beneficial to others and pave the way to a better world, a task that Leo Baeck sees himself accomplishing by repairing his lost and wounded community and Jung by writing about evil and continuing his practice as a wounded healer.

The play doesn't ask that we embrace or forgive the protagonists, but that we follow Woman's gentle hand as she guides them toward a deeper understanding of who they are and gives the audience an opportunity to grasp what only an inner perspective can fathom. We were not there, we were not they, and we cannot judge the past from the perspective of present morality. Yet we can engage with the questions raised. We can even ask ourselves where and when in our own lives we might have acted as they did, and only then can a deeply needed forgiveness be found.

The character of Woman taught me not to judge, assign guilt, or defend either of them but to engage with shadow, move through it and emerge with a heart that has seen otherness and forgiven. Playing her in this way was hugely rewarding to me. I felt like the container of the action, a backdrop to the drama of existence, moved impersonally by the struggles of the characters, yet emanating from a freer perspective. This reflection on the limitations inherent in the human, oh so human field, leaves me a little humbler. Living in the gray zone reconciles us with our flawed, blind, and fearful nature, and holding this awareness with compassion reminds us that we, too, are also, at times, capable of integrity, light, and courage.

# Music for "The Analyst and the Rabbi"

### By Barbara Helen Miller

The musical interludes for the cast's previous performance of "Scenes from *The Red Book*" were recorded improvisations that the guitarist Wim de Vrij and I had made on one fine Sunday in a sound studio. When Murray Stein asked me if I would consider participating in the next play with some cello pieces, my first idea was along similar lines, to record improvisations. Then, at the IAAP Congress in Kyoto (2016), Henry Abramovitch approached me with the invitation to provide music for the new play he was writing with Murray Stein, and he mentioned the intense cultural activity in Theresienstadt (concentration camp where Rabbi Baeck was interned). This set me on the path to find music composed in Theresienstadt that would be appropriate between the scenes of the play. After perusing several compositions, I settled on the opera "The Emperor of Atlantis or The Disobedience of Death" by Viktor Ullmann with a libretto by Peter Kien, which used the idea, from the Grimm fairy tale *The Peasant's Wise Daughter,* of witty exchanges. There are some fine performances of the opera that can be viewed on YouTube, and after listening I could extract motifs to be used for 1) terror and confusion, 2) Sabina Spielrein, and 3) love and pain of separation. The musical motif for Rabbi Baeck I found in Beethoven's String Quartet op 18, # 6, "La Malinconia." The *journey* of Jung and Baeck's meeting I found in Vivaldi's Cello Sonata #6; the *movement of soul* in Boccherini's Cello Concerto in B flat Major, adagio; Jung's moment of insight and his taking of *responsibility* in J.S. Bach's Johannes Passion, Aria # 58 "Es ist vollbracht."

The play came alive during rehearsals when I heard the lines spoken, and I placed my musical response accordingly. We (the whole crew, consisting of Murray, Henry, Paul, John, Dariane and Jan) worked together, considering the length and placement of each musical section so that it should work effectively for that dramatic moment. During the performances, my experience was that of involvement in the emotional impact of the encounter onstage, and I felt glad to be uttering (through music) something so basic and gripping as the search of soul taking place on stage.

My journey started with listening to Ullman and Kien's opera from Theresienstadt, "Der Kaiser von Atlantis." It should be mentioned that just as important as the music is the libretto. Interned in Theresienstadt in 1941, Kien was officially the director of the Technical Drawing Office of the Jewish Self Administration. He sketched many depictions of living conditions in the ghetto. His drawings are among the most important works documenting that Theresienstadt was (definitely) *not* the model Jewish settlement the Nazis portrayed to outsiders. His drawings accurately reflect that its inhabitants were confined in inhuman conditions and treated severely. In "Der Kaiser von Atlantis," Kien made a satire of Hitler, showing the Kaiser as being far removed from human contact and delivering an order for "total war." Acting in another sphere are Death and Harlequin. When Death hears the Kaiser's plan for total war, Death refuses to "take" anyone. Due to there being no death, the whole situation starts to change. Soldiers become more interested in flirting with lovely ladies, who respond in turn, than with carrying on this (now truly) senseless killing. The Kaiser becomes frustrated and demands a change. When the Kaiser and Death start to negotiate, Harlequin utters this intriguing line: "Death becomes a poet when he becomes at one with love." The Kaiser finally agrees to Death's conditions, which include that he must be the first to be taken by Death. With my involvement with an opera that would have been discussed among those interned at Theresienstadt, I felt I was coming close to Rabbi Baeck, who was interned there. The humor and subtle shifts in plot in "Der Kaiser von Atlantis" show an amazing life spirit. When I told the last line to my 85-year-old friend who grew up in Amsterdam, he laughed out loud at the final scene titled, "Death's condition to take up his work again being that the Kaiser shall be the first taken by Death," commenting: "Great humor." My friend was in school with Anne Frank, and he remembers playing with her in front of their homes. He has up-close experiences that give him an immediate recognition and delight in this "inside joke."

The emotional climax for me at each performance was when I played Bach's "Es ist vollbracht" ("It is accomplished"). This aria comes immediately after Jesus's final words on the cross, "Es ist vollbracht," and right before the Evangelist announces Jesus's death. I used for inspiration the 1985 performance by Concentus Musicus Wien and the Tölzer Knabenchor, directed by Nikolaus Harnoncourt, soloists Panito Iconomou (alto) and Christophe Coin (playing the viola da gamba). It is still on YouTube. What can be felt is that Iconomou was in a "flow" (he also expressed this experience in an interview) as well as was Christophe Coin (playing the viola da gamba). They made magic. This performance remains the single most cited for "Es ist vollbracht," which one can appreciate when this truly exceptional "flow" is heard.

Bach based his St. John's Passion on Pietist August Hermann Francke's sermons, for which he got into trouble with the Leipzig orthodox Lutheran magistrates (see Baron 2006). The issue is and was religious experience. Here is a slice of text from Gardiner (2014) *Bach, Music in the Castle of Heaven*, wherein the issue is made clear: "The preface of a Pietist hymnal of 1733 gives specific instructions for its readers and singers to experience the emotions depicted by inspired hymnists so that 'he seizes all of the Psalms' powers and motions in himself and begins to sing as if the songs are not strange to him, but rather as if he had composed them himself, as his own prayer produced with the deeper sensations of his heart.'" (Ibid. pg. 34).

The text:

> It is accomplished
> What comfort for all suffering souls!
> The night of sorrow
> Now reaches its final hours.
> The hero from Judah triumphs in his might
> And brings the strife to an end.
> It is accomplished!

Additionally I experienced solace during the Vivaldi excerpts. They tie the performance together, being played at the beginning and end, and they show the steady movement forward that I imagine Baeck and Jung to have done.

What I have shared here are some of my thoughts while compiling the music, while practicing alone, while rehearsing and while performing. My sense of musical performance is that these many thoughts and/or emotions are communicated, perhaps viscerally registered, during a performance.

# References

Baron, Carol K. (2006) *Bach's Changing World, Voices in the Community.* Rochester, NY: University of Rochester Press.

Gardiner, John Eliot (2014) *Bach, Music in the Castle of Heaven.* New York: Alfred A. Knopf.

J.S. Bach - Johannes-Passion - Es ist vollbracht - alto aria – YouTube
https://www.youtube.com/watch?v=K_QAoanXntw

Der Kaiser von Atlantis (Viktor Ullmann) - Teatro Colón 2006 (Completa) - YouTube https://www.youtube.com/watch?v=EJNN_YlLtd4

# Appendix

Correspondence between C. G. Jung and Rabbi Leo Baeck
ETH Jung Archives

- Leo Baeck to C.G. Jung, 4 Dec. 1930 (ETH University Archives identification code: Hs 1056: 543)
- Secretary C.G. Jung to Leo Baeck, 7 Oct. 1946 (Hs 1056: 12905)
- Secretary C.G. Jung to Leo Baeck, 8 Oct. 1946 (Hs 1056: 12906)
(translated by Murray Stein)

Reproduced by permission of the Foundation of the Works of C.G. Jung, Zurich

1.
Berlin, den 4. Dezember 1930

Sehr geehrter Herr Dr. Jung,
   Nach ihrem Vortrag in Darmstadt habe ich Sie leider nicht mehr erreichen können, ich hätte Ihnen gern sofort gedankt. So sollen diese Zeilen meiner Dank zu Ihnen bringen.
   Er kommt aus herzlichem Empfinden hervor, für vieles Frühere auch an Ihnen. Ihre Schriften über Psychologie sind

mir seit Jahren in meinen religionspsychologischen Vorlesungen und Übungen ein Unentbehrliches.

So war es mir doppelt eine Freude, Sie nun zu sehen und zu hören.

Mit besten Empfehlungen bin ich,

Ihr ergebener,

Leo Baeck

Berlin, 4 December 1930

Dear Dr. Jung,

If I had been able to reach you after your speech in Darmstadt, I would have liked to thank you immediately. So these lines are meant to offer you my thanks.

This comes to you also with heartfelt feeling for much in the past. Your writings on psychology have been indispensable to me for years in my religious psychology lectures and exercises.

So it was twice the pleasure to see and hear you at this time.

With best wishes, I am,

Yours faithfully,

Leo Baeck

2.
den 7. Oktober 1946

> Herrn Dr. Leo Baeck
> c/o Dr. Mell,
> Villa Lucia,
> Lugano-Cassarate

Sehr geehrter Herr Doktor,
Im Auftrag von Herrn Prof. Jung möchte ich Ihnen nochmals bestätigen, dass er Sie sehr gerne nächsten Sonntag (13.X) zum Thé erwartet. Ohne Gegenbericht Ihrerseits wird man Sie, ca. 16:45 im Hotel Baur en Ville in Zürich mit dem Auto abholen.

> Mit vorzüglicher Hochachtung,
> Ihre ergebene
> Sekretärin

October 7, 1946

> Dr. Leo Baeck
> c / o Dr. med. Mell,
> Villa Lucia, Lugano-Cassarate

Dear Doctor,
On behalf of Prof. Jung I would like to confirm once again that he would very much like to see you next Sunday (13.X) for tea. Without an objection on your part, you will be picked up at about 16:45 at the Hotel Baur en Ville in Zurich by car.

> Yours sincerely,
> With devotion,
> Secretary

3.

den 8. Oktober 1946

> Herrn Dr. Leo Baeck
> c/o Dr. Mell
> Villa Lucia
> Lugano-Cassarate

Sehr geehrter Herr Doktor,

Wie Herr Prof. Jung durch Frau Dr. Katzenstein erfuhr, werden Sie Sonntag Nachmittag schwer abkömmlich sein. Er bittet mich nun, Ihnen mitzuteilen, dass es ihn und Frau Prof. Jung sehr freuen würde, wenn Sie statt zum Thé zum Nachtessen nach Küsnacht kommen könnten. Dürfte ich Sie wohl um eine gelegentliche Mitteilung bitten, wo man Sie ca. 7 Uhr in Zürich abholen darf?

> Mit vorzüglicher Hochachtung,
> Ihre ergebene
> Sekretärin

October 8, 1946

> Dr. Leo Baeck
> c / o Dr. med. Mell Villa Lucia
> Lugano-Cassarate

Dear Doctor,

As Prof. Jung has learned from Dr. Katzenstein, you will be difficult to reach on Sunday afternoon. He now asks me to inform you that he and Mrs. Prof. Jung would be very happy if you could come to Küsnacht for dinner instead of tea. May I ask you for a message, where you can be picked you up around 7 clock in Zurich?

Yours sincerely,

With devotion,

Secretary

# Bibliography

Abramovitch, Henry (2016) "The Search for a New Ethic: Professional and Clinical Dilemmas," in *Turbulent Times, Creative Minds: Erich Neumann and C.G. Jung in Relationship (1933-1960)*, Asheville, NC: Chiron Publications, pp. 167-184.

Arendt, Hannah (2006) *Eichmann in Jerusalem,* London: Penguin Books.

Baker, Leonard (1978) *Days of Sorrow and Pain: Leo Baeck and the Berlin Jews*, New York: Macmillan Publishing Co.

Baeck, Leo (1948) "Individuum ineffabile," in *Eranos Jahrbuch* 1947, Zurich: Rhein-Verlag.

Baeck, Leo (1949) "A People Stands Before Its God," in *We Survived: The Stories of Fourteen of the Hidden and the Hunted of Nazi Germany*, as told to Eric H. Boehm, New Haven: Yale University Press.

Baeck, Leo (1965) *This People Israel: The Meaning of Jewish Existence*, translated by Albert H. Friedlander, London: W.H. Allen.

Bair, Deirdre (2006) *Jung, A Biography*, Boston, New York, London: Little, Brown and Company.

Buber, Martin (1952; 1988) *Eclipse of God: Studies in the Relation between Religion and Philosophy*, Atlantic Highlands, NJ: International Humanities Press.

Friedlander, Albert (1992) *Leo Baeck: Teacher of Theresienstadt*, New York: Overlook Press.

Jaffé, Aniela (1989) *From the Life and Work of C.G. Jung*, Einsiedeln: Daimon Verlag.

Jung, C.G. (1934/1964) "The State of Psychotherapy Today," in *Collected Works of C.G. Jung*, Vol. 10, Princeton, NJ: Princeton University Press.

Jung, C.G. (1961) *Memories, Dreams, Reflections*, New York: Vintage Books.

Jung, C.G. (1973) *Letters*, Vol. 1, edited by Gerhard Adler, Princeton, NJ: Princeton University Press.

Jung, C.G. (2009) *The Red Book: Liber Novus*, edited by Sonu Shamdasani, New York: W.W. Norton & Company.

Knott, Marie Louise (ed.) (2017) *The Correspondence of Hannah Arendt and Gershom Scholem*. Translated by Anthony David. Chicago, IL: University of Chicago Press.

Liebscher, Martin (ed.) (2016) *Analytical Psychology in Exile: The Correspondence of C.G. Jung and Erich Neumann*, Princeton, NJ: Princeton University Press.

Maidenbaum, Aryeh and Stephen Martin (eds.) (1991) *Lingering Shadows: Jungians, Freudians, and Anti-Semitism*, Boston and London: Shambhala Publications.

Maidenbaum, Aryeh (ed.) (2002) *Jung and the Shadow of Anti-Semitism*, Berwick, ME: Nicolas-Hayes.

Schoenl, W. and L. (2016) *Jung's Evolving Views of Nazi Germany: From the Nazi Takeover to the End of World War II*, Asheville, NC: Chiron Publications.

Shalit, Erel and Murray Stein (eds.) (2016) *Turbulent Times, Creative Minds: Erich Neumann and C.G. Jung in Relationship* (1933-1960), Asheville, NC: Chiron Publications.

Shehadeh, Raja (2017) *Where the Line is Drawn: Crossing Boundaries in Occupied Palestine*, London: Profile Books.

Stein, Murray (2016) "Erich Neumann and C.G. Jung on 'The Problem of Evil," in *Turbulent Times, Creative Minds: Erich Neumann and C.G. Jung in Relationship* (1933-1960), Asheville, NC: Chiron Publications, pp. 185-196.